NO EXCUSES

T.C. Squires

This is a work of nonfiction based on true events. Names, characters, places, and incidents are used factually and represent real individuals and occurrences. Any coincidental resemblance to other persons or events is entirely unintentional. Excerpts written from the perspective of the author are included in the book. These excerpts represent the author's personal experiences and reflections on the events portrayed. They are intended to provide insight and perspective into the narrative.

No Excuses is a work of creative nonfiction, presenting real-life events and experiences as perceived and intrepreted by the author. The author has made every effort to ensure the accuracy of the information presented, relying on a variety of sources, including personal recollections, research, and documentation. However, minor details may have been adjusted for the purposes of storytelling and narrative flow.

The author expresses deep gratitude for the opportunity to share their own story through this book. The author's personal experiences and perspectives form the basis of the narrative, providing insight into the events depicted. The names of individuals and places have been used factually, with no pseudonyms or alterations for privacy.

Quotes from various news articles are used in this book and are cited in the Appendix. The quotes have been reproduced accurately with some corrections in brackets [ ], and are acknowledged to the best of the author's knowledge. The inclusion of these quotes does not imply endorsement by the individuals or organizations mentioned. Photo credit is given in the Appendix as known.

ISBN:
Printed in the United States of America
1st Edition Paperback June 2023

For permissions and inquiries, please contact:
T.C. Squires
sbmaximization@gmail.com

Note: While every precaution has been taken in the preparation of this book, the author and the publisher assume no responsibility for errors or omissions, or for damages from the use of the information contained herin.

Cover design by: T.C. Squires
Cover image: The Voice of Amateur Baseball

Dedicated to the Sylvan Hills Bears Community
in Memory of Taylor Roark, Dwight Turpin,
Bill Blackwood, and Jerry Tipton.

*"High school is your chance to build character, dedicate yourself to something you love, achieve your ultimate goal, overcome deceitful propaganda, and overall, it's your chance to **define Yourself!**"*

~ Bonnie Brown, SHHS Senior 2008

CONTENTS

PREFACE

There is a reason the greatest authors and essayists have more often than not chosen baseball for their topic.

It is a game that lends itself to eloquence better than any of the other sports. Football is a slog through the mud; basketball a frenetic box of chaos. But baseball is graceful and expansive. Just gazing down on an empty diamond settles the mind.

From the crisp dignity of its uniforms to the fluidity of its unimpeded players moving about the field to its languid (literally) timeless pace, it is a game that quietly excites the heart. Football may awaken your inner beast, basketball might stir the blood into a froth.

But baseball – when played exquisitely and with just the right dash of drama – has a quality about it that almost has to speak for itself. (Poorly played, by the way, it can be a maddening thing to watch, very nearly an insult to the senses. Which is why, when people ask me my favorite sport to cover, I hesitate to say it is baseball. Yet, it is.)

It is a game that rewards attention to detail. It may be scoreless in the third inning, but did you notice that their pitcher is starting to work behind in the count? That he is starting to leave his curve ball up a little? Aren't the batters starting to make better swings the second time through the lineup?

Perhaps that is why writers have struggled so mightily over the years to capture the soul bliss it can on rare occasion confer upon us.[2]

CHAPTER 1

Sunday, August 19, 2007

I got the call a few days before. Meet at Casey's house. Don't block anyone's driveway. Bring money or toilet paper.

To be honest, I wasn't typically one to get this kind of invitation. None of my closest friends were going to be there. Nonetheless, I was excited to take part in something I had only heard about in movies or after the first day of school.

I pulled up to the line of cars down the street. There were twenty or thirty of us, mainly athletes and cheerleaders, to take part in the annual tradition of rolling the junior class. We gathered in Casey's driveway, snapped a quick photo to prove we were there, and the ladies laid out the plan. Everyone was to consolidate vehicles and meet at the first house not too far away, then we would snake our way across Sherwood and North Little Rock. I was wary of driving my car which was adorned with blue and white window chalk that read *"SENIOR,"* which might as well have said *"ARREST ME."*

I jumped in the bed of one of the pickups filled with toilet paper – probably not my smartest decision—and we set out. If we needed to roll someone on the move, I was ready. We actually ran into a group of seniors from NLR, who I promptly pelted through their open car windows. One by one, we hit house after house of sleeping juniors, trying to make as little noise as possible and staying away from the numerous Sherwood police cars. Silly string, Vaseline, and shaving cream made unexpected appearances as we covered yards, trees, vehicles, and driveways.

Before the night was over the following seniors were taken to the police station: Abby McAdams, Jacob Clark, Lane Goff, and Deyonté Davis. However, being arrested did not stop these seniors from finishing out the night with their friends. They met back up with everyone and ended the night having fun. Senior Lane Goff said, "I didn't really care about being arrested. It was actually fun since we didn't get in much trouble!"[3]

We realized a few hours in that there was no way we were going to be able to roll every house on the list and still get some sleep. Midnight arrived, and I received a phone call from my dad. He was angry because I hadn't made it home yet since it was past Sherwood's student curfew. I told my chauffeur that I needed to be dropped off at Walmart. Dad picked me up and took me back to Casey's house, and he insisted on driving my car home.

On Sunday, August 19, many of the Sylvan Hills High School seniors of 2008 met at Casey Jeu's to continue the grand tradition of senior roll night. It was nearing 10:30 when the chaos began, with nearly 20 cars parading to the underclassmen's houses to begin the "welcome back" terror from the seniors.

Junior Casey Cerrato was one of the chosen that the seniors rolled. When asked about the experience, he replied, "My first thought was that I was going to have to clean the mess. But, when I saw all my friends, I wasn't mad or anything."

Senior roll night is the first of several special events for the seniors to celebrate the beginning of the end. The seniors get together to map out a night of mischief to cover the underclassmen yards and cars with harmless things like silly string, forks, saran wrap, car paint, and a whole lot of toilet paper.

Some junior parents got upset with all the toilet paper and cars in their front yard and contacted the police. However, only one car full of seniors were actually taken to the Sherwood police department and forced to call adults to come get them.

One parent of a senior felt a need to strike out in support of the tradition. Gwynnann Turpin, whose son Mark is a senior, said "This celebration is one night out of the whole year. It is a chance for the seniors to say 'hey we made it let's celebrate and have some good clean fun.' It's not like these kids are driving around shooting guns, breaking glass, and slashing tires. It's toilet paper. Be proud of these kids and their achievements."[4]

None of us got much sleep that night, especially with the Senior parade early Monday morning. I was definitely groggy as I drove down Highway 107 with the rest of our class, all the way up Bear Paw Road to the school parking spots we had claimed by decorating with spray-painted names and designs.

Another year, another opportunity. On August 20th, classmates were reunited for the first day of school. Soon club meetings and sporting events took place, class projects began, and the Grizz Zone tried to uphold its previous standards; interaction had begun. Everyone scrambled to get their schedules changed in order to get out of classes they didn't need or want and into those that would help build their character. In fact, so many students requested alterations that everyone was required to pick up a whole new schedule even if it had not been changed.

Athletes were working hard and putting in time, effort, and dedication into the sports they played to get on top. There were also many new faces in the hallways and in the classrooms. Not only was it necessary to welcome the freshmen, but also the abundance of new teachers. It was a great achievement to make everyone feel at home. One person making sure to call Sylvan Hills home was Mr. Ebbs who retained his position as principal (the first repeat in 5 years). He didn't buy into the implied propaganda of going "one-and-done."

SYLVAN HILLS HIGH SCHOOL

Monday morning started slow, like most Mondays, with the usual waiting in line on Bear Paw Road while parents dragged their scarcely awake children to the front of the school. It was easy to tell which cars were driven by students based on how often they honked. Patience was a learned trait that didn't sink in until the end of junior year, then was tested endlessly over the year until that cap and gown came in.

The school grounds were mediocre: gray-tan brick, windowless walls and cracked cement patios with ghosts of pressure-washed graffiti. A single pine tree sat in the middle of the campus courtyard, which hardly qualified as sylvan. The main building, dedicated in 1967 and hardly updated in the 40 years since, was a bleak and hopeless place designed like the very prisons to which many students would one day enter. Trailers were one of the few additions. Although they weren't visible from the main road, we knew them all too well. It can't really be said that they were exciting, but at least they didn't contain asbestos like the classrooms of the now-condemned 1920s middle school, which we attended a few short years ago. The elementary school was just a short walk away, too. Arkansas wasn't been known for its success in education. We, as students, would regularly make fun of the old buildings, equipment, and lack of funding. Our history books ended with George H.W. Bush as President. The multiple district superintendents making six figures were also part of the problem. There was even a situation one year at the Sylvan Hills versus North Little Rock football game where part of the visiting bleachers collapsed. Never mind the number of police officers required to keep students from the two schools apart during the game. Fights still somehow managed to break out. High school was a strange place.

School rankings come out by the dozens every year and Arkansas lands all across the spectrum, making it hard to draw much elation or sorrow from any of them. We have to look just as philosophically at the latest one, which ranks the quality of Arkansas public schools no lower than eighth in the country, but it offers at least some medium-sized encouragement.

The 12th annual Quality Counts report by Education Week, the Washington-based journal on American education, gave Arkansas a B-minus for the overall quality of its education, a little better than the nation as a whole, which got a C. Arkansas in the past has been down there with the below-average states. Neighboring Mississippi, our longtime ally in the basement, is still there. It was among six states with a D minus.

But here is why the report is encouraging: The measurements of education policies, such as standards, accountability and spending, where Arkansas has made dramatic strides in the past four years, ought to reflect the quality of future learning.

Arkansas ranked highest, second among the 50 states and the District of Columbia, in teacher quality, a B plus. Arkansas teachers must follow a rigorous licensing process, compensation was raised sharply and the state provides mentoring programs and a variety of professional development opportunities. Only a few years ago Arkansas ranked 49th or 50th in teacher salaries but now only Texas of the surrounding states pays teachers more on average.[6]

Students parked in the large main lot next to the football field, while teachers parked close to the 300 building. They also used a lot in front of the school next to the road that led into the Sylvan Hills Optimist. A circle drive near the office facilitated quick loading and unloading as parents dropped off their kids. Crowds and cliques of people stood in the open courtyard outside the gym, waiting for the 8:30 bell to ring or for a fight to break out. Despite the presence of several resource officers and rent-a-cops, we never knew which one we were going to get. Students used to call in bomb threats from the school payphone just to get out of class, but the threats had become serious enough to warrant extra security.

Or, we'd sit in the cafeteria, rushing through the homework we forgot or refused to do the night before. There was a domino effect: first-period homework was done before school, second-period homework was done during the first period, and so on. Most of my friend group were in the same classes, and our homework became group work, regardless of how it was assigned.

Students were then forced into a habitual seven-period-a-day routine of class, class, class, class, lunch, class, class, class. It was our third different schedule in as many years. The district tried block scheduling, then modified block, and now seven-period days. The constant changes eventually put the school in a bind, as some graduating students would not have enough time slots to get the credits they needed to graduate. Principal Danny Ebbs, in his second year, would endup taking on this problem head-on with the Pulaski County Special School District (PCSSD) Board.

My first-period class was AP European History with Mrs. Evans. She was one of the most animated teachers I'd ever had. Whether it was her excitement for teaching as she slammed her fist on the podium, the shirtless Dwayne *"The Rock"* Johnson poster hanging on the whiteboard, her constant mumbling behind her desk about the number of different classes the school had her teaching right before she retired while we worked on the *"Neely Plan,"* or watching a late Tucker Weatherford army crawl through the door to his desk so he wasn't counted tardy, it was by far the best class to start the day in. My best friend Russell, whom I'd been friends with since birth, sat behind me with the rest of our crew circling us. The fifty-minute periods plus time for announcements usually went by fast.

After the bell, we'd hustle downstairs, our heavy backpacks dangling to our waists, to Mr. Johnson's AP Chemistry class. This was by far the most intensive class. Johnson was teaching as he would teach his college classes, covering atomic structure, molecular compounds, and kinetics. I enjoyed the class so much that I've kept my composition notebooks even to this day. The class was split across two periods for lab purposes. I'd usually head up the stairs to the 300 building to buy a snack from Mr. Rushing to hold me over until lunch. Another fifty minutes of watching Mr. Johnson blow tiles out of the drop ceiling or show us the properties of light, and then we were off to AP English.

Mrs. Young was perhaps the most composed and level-headed of all my teachers, or perhaps it was just that retirement was imminent. Either way, I struggled to remain alert through the poems, plays, and essays as my muscles and stomach protested from an early morning workout. Her class was a priority solely because we required it to graduate, but leaving it on time was more important because we needed all the time possible to go grab lunch and return to school. I believe, at the time, that Arkansas law did not permit students to depart campus for any reason other than work programs or athletics. However, due to the size of Sylvan Hills' student population, the cafeteria could not accommodate all students across two lunch periods. Even with three lunches a few years later, it was still challenging. A compromise was eventually reached that allowed seniors and juniors with excellent grades and conduct to leave school for lunch.

Off campus lunch had many advantages and disadvantages. The good thing about leaving for lunch was that cafeteria food was not the everyday choice. Also, long lines were something [to] be avoided, and there were just [too] many rules in the cafeteria.

There were, however, problems leaving campus for lunch. Jacob Davis needed more time to get somewhere and back in thirty minutes. Brian Davis agreed that students needed more than thirty minutes so as not to speed getting back to class on time.

Another disadvantage was how expensive it was to buy fast food [every day]. Kaitlin Edwards said she spent about four dollars a day on food and Saif Rehman spent about five or six dollars. This meant that students were spending twenty to twenty-five dollars a week on lunch alone.[7]

Eric, Jared, Russell, Blake, and I used to drive to the Walmart deli to grab chicken strips, potato wedges, and fried okra. Before we had cars, we walked to the Subway down the street from school. Then, we returned to campus to eat lunch in Mr. Dare's room before our fifth-period AP Calculus class.

I can still hear him saying *"Do the math!"* from the whiteboard as we asked question after question. I love solving puzzles. To me, that's all math was: one big puzzle after another. However, there was something about Calculus that I wasn't prepared for. I don't want to blame Mr. Dare because he was an excellent teacher, and blaming my senioritis is a lame excuse since I performed well in all of my other classes. But, Calculus was a challenge for me. Things started to come together towards the end of the second semester, but exigent circumstances changed that later in the year.

During sixth period, we had AP Music Theory with Mrs. Harris, the choir director. That was her main focus throughout the year. Choir. Our small group, consisting of a subset the same students as our other AP classes, spent more time playing Farkle than we ever did studying Music Theory. Or maybe the material just came easy to us. I played the piano, the twins were in the band, Jody and Susana were musically inclined, and the rest of the class had a similar background. Chord progressions and ancient musical texts seemed like nothing to fret about.

Technically, the school day went on for another fifty minutes, but my curriculum-based classes ended there. I don't even know what classes my friends were taking or what classes were offered during seventh period. I had baseball. At least a quarter of the school had athletics to end the day. So, I would head off to the football fieldhouse or down to the baseball field depending on the time of year to finish up my day. Then, there was the same line of cars after school. Students raced to the light at the end of Bear Paw before traffic clogged with buses. It was the same monotonous routine every day, well, for most.

Dennis Dare

mathematics

Do the math!
Dennis Dare

Let's rewind a few hours. Before the buses began picking up students, before the roads got busy, and while Shipley's Donuts just switched on their "OPEN" sign. Well before the start of the school day, while most of the student body lay in bed, waiting for their alarms to go off so they could hit the snooze button three or four times, I was already up and on my way to the fieldhouse.

Reluctantly, my blue and tan GMC with SENIOR written across the back glass started. It was as if the car knew what time it was. The heat was already blasting as I hoped to thaw my frozen hands. A thin layer of ice covered the windshield. Thoughts ran through my mind—why was I doing this? I had to find the ice scraper while the car warmed up enough to drive. It must have been the coldest day of the year; it's hard to know since the news wouldn't come on for another fifteen minutes. Slowly backing out of the driveway, so as not to disturb the rest of the household, it was a short drive to school - eight minutes on a regular day with traffic, but right now, maybe five.

There was nothing good on the radio, so I played the CD that was in the player—TobyMac's Renovating Diverse City. *"The Slam"* was the perfect song for the occasion. I was headed to our 6:00 am workout on the chilly November morning. We hadn't had tryouts yet, but after our showing in the State Tournament over the last two years, we had no time to waste. This was baseball.

I won't lie; most mornings, I didn't want to be there. What eighteen-year-old wants to be at school two hours before the bell rings? I would choose extra sleep any day over this, especially after a late night at church or practice. Now, hear me out—team building and working out were great. There were much worse things a high school senior could get into. Everything just blurred together when your face was numb, and you were running a mile in the dark. You didn't want to be late for workouts; it wasn't pretty. The next day, you'd have to be at the fieldhouse even earlier to do sprints by yourself with Coach standing at the fence with his hot coffee and ear warmers. It only happened a few times, mostly with rookies, but they learned quickly.

I finally arrived and parked close to the building, then walked into the almost full room. The fieldhouse was pretty cramped. Coach talked for a bit, laying out the exercises for the morning. Then, we'd circle up for our stretching routine. Someone, usually a senior or two, would take the center of the circle to call out the stretches and count off the time.

Standing up, with arms straight out to your sides parallel to the floor, start with fifteen seconds of small circling motions forward. Follow with fifteen seconds of small circles backward. Then move on to big circles forward to stretch out the whole shoulder, and repeat backward. In the same position, with arms out straight, do fifteen seconds of quick up-down movements about three inches away from center. Follow this with fifteen seconds of shoulder press and then fifteen seconds of bench press. At this point, the burn usually kicks in, so move on to lateral-raise overhead flies. Rix added a flailing arm-crossing motion across the chest. Then, with your bent arms out to the side, do a standing lumbar rotation side to side and finish with fifteen seconds of small circles forward and backward again. This warm-up routine should take about three minutes to complete.

Next up, stretch your legs. Start with fifteen seconds of feet together and stretch your hamstrings by touching your toes. Then, cross your right leg over and repeat, followed by the left leg. While still standing, with legs spread apart, go straight down to the floor, stretching to the right leg, then to the left side. In the middle, do chops in front, straight down, and back. For deep squat stretches, push your knees apart for fifteen seconds, which could sometimes turn into a headstand contest. Take a seat with legs out front, touching your toes for ten seconds. Legs split apart, go down to the right, then to the left. Cross your right leg for a seated glute stretch, then repeat with the left leg. That was it for solo stretches unless you wanted to add in a frog pose like D.J. Then, pair up for team stretches. Daulton wasn't pleased to see that I was the last one without a partner, as this usually happened that way. *"Come on, TC,"* he'd say. Stretch your shoulders by doing a cross-armed push and pull stretch, then your triceps by putting both arms behind your back and pushing up towards the shoulders. Finish with calf and quad stretches, and anything else you need to do personally before starting. If you were on the ball field, finish with a light jog to center field and back before starting to throw.

We did this warm-up routine before every workout, every practice, and every game. It was ingrained in my memory from day one as a freshman, warming up after school on Field 5 above the high school field while the Varsity team was practicing. At this point in our career, we had probably done this routine over a thousand times. Consistency, stamina, and strength were what was going to make us a championship team.

From there, we would split into our workout groups, usually consisting of two or three people depending on the available space. The fieldhouse wasn't particularly roomy with 9th through 12th graders using it. Half of the space was occupied by football equipment and lockers, while the rest was taken up by weight benches and racks. All the coaches had to squeeze into a small office. There were approximately ten racks with old, beat-up benches and rusted weights. The padded floor had permanent dents in some areas. We opened all the doors and turned on the one fan, attempting to air out the stench left by unwashed football pads and workout equipment that was probably older than we were. Even though it was cold outside, it was worth it. Sharing the weight room had always been difficult, but soon we'd be working out at the new indoor facility. We hoped. That had been the story for at least three or four years. Until then, this was our place too. Some days we rotated stations, while other days we stuck to one rack. Full-body workouts were the norm, with legs, arms, abs, back, legs again, and stretching. The pain was constant and consistent.

An hour or so later, we were exhausted. Bed never sounded so good. If only that were a possibility. We still had classes to attend, which didn't seem like a priority, especially as a Senior with only a few credits left. After a workout like this, I'd be lucky if I could hold a pencil or move my arms in first period. Some of the guys returned home for a quick shower and donuts if the line wasn't too long, but I couldn't see how they could hold the steering wheel. We'd wander our way into the courtyard or cafeteria with the rest of the student body to get ready for the bell, without most students even knowing we'd been there since 6:00 am. It was what made us different. Just another day.

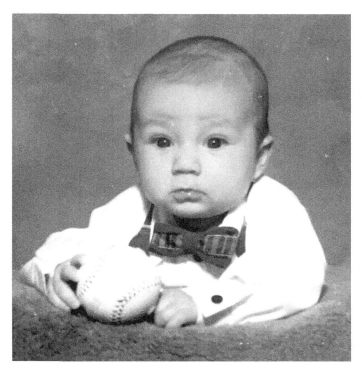

As a single-sport athlete, baseball was everything to me. I dedicated most of my life to the sport, even quitting my job of two-years at Academy Sports & Outdoors to focus solely on it. Dad didn't approve of the job anyway, so he was surprised but not opposed when I told him about my decision. Despite a city-wide curfew in Sherwood at midnight for anyone still in school, some of my bosses were terrible about locking us in too late, so quitting was the right choice.

According to a family friend, my love for baseball began as early as two years old, hitting with a plastic bat and ball at the ballpark while my dad played softball. T-ball championships and All-Star travel ball throughout the summer were typical. Our family vacations often centered around baseball tournaments. If

I were to add up the hours spent playing, practicing, traveling, or working out for baseball leading up to my senior year, it would equal several full years of my life.

My fall semester of senior year was no different. After AP Music Theory, I was released for baseball until the 3:50 pm bell. We stayed way past 3:50 pm, of course. While about half of the team played football, the rest of us spent the fall lifting weights, running circuits, and throwing weight balls against a plywood board in our partially finished indoor facility. After years of the steel building laying in the back of the little league parking lot, concrete had been poured, the frame constructed, and some walls were attached with a roof. Turf, cages, and weights hadn't been moved in, yet, but they were coming.

Coach Chris Foor's blue pickup with the *Foor4Four* license plate parked outside the fieldhouse every day was a change from previous years when Coach Verdell was in charge of off-season workouts. Coach V was laid-back and fairly generous. A lot of the time, he was more focused on the golf team, though on occasion, he'd follow our runs on his bike to make sure we weren't walking. His retirement from coaching baseball the previous year gave way for Foor to step in as Tipton's Assistant baseball coach. Coach Tyson Norseworthy took over some of Foor's old duties in between coaching football and teaching at the middle school. Foor was still new to Sylvan Hills baseball, but he had the drive to win, and that's what mattered, for the most part. If only he would put on a shirt when working out in the fieldhouse and brag less about his college baseball days and traveling softball team. I get it; he was trying to fit in with the team and be one of the guys. McKinney and Dillon weren't against goofing off with him, but I wasn't a fan of his humor.

On Mondays, Wednesdays, and Fridays, we lifted weights, doing bench presses, cleans, rows, push-ups, curls, squats, dips, and lunges. We did sets and sets and sets, but there wasn't a daily workout plan, only a basic outline. Supervision was similar, which may explain why there were so many injuries that offseason. I strained my back while running, and my left shoulder during a pull-up workout. Perez dropped 185 lbs on his chest during bench press as his spotter wasn't paying enough attention. When his arms gave out, the bar cracked his sternum in half. J.T. broke his foot, which was entirely unrelated to off-season workouts as he broke it during a pick-up game of basketball, but it's worth mentioning. After that, Coach Tipton banned us from playing unsanctioned games of any sport, as we couldn't afford to lose anyone long-term.

Tuesdays were the most challenging workouts of the week. We typically began with circuits, followed by hill sprints.

There were two circuits: a small one and a large one. Both involved running from the fieldhouse around the student parking lot towards the baseball fields. The small circuit turned off around the T-ball fields, went down to the elementary school, all the way to Highway 107, ran to Bear Paw Road, and then circled back to the fieldhouse, covering about three miles. The large circuit went all the way to the softball fields, then to Woody's Sherwood Forest, and back to the baseball field before following the same path down to Highway 107 and Bear Paw as the small circuit. It was at least another two or three miles, all of which involved running up and down hills. Hence the name Sylvan Hills Bears, or as we were otherwise known, the Hillside Bears.

Thursdays consisted of a timed mile run around the track, followed by more hill sprints. Coach Foor insisted that we beat our previous week's time, or else we had to show up to school early the next day to run it again. I don't know how many players ended up with that punishment, but I didn't want to find out. Early in the fall, I was terrible at running and usually started too fast, which strained my back. As a result, I learned to match Ty Van Schyock's pace for the first three laps to finish on time. Later in the fall, I started a targeted running program and told Foor that I would be focusing on it, not running at school. I can't say he was pleased, but I wasn't a huge fan of Coach Foor anyway. I didn't care. My dad was paying for me to train alongside some of the state's top high school, college, and pro athletes at BJ Maack's Arkansas Sports Performance Center. I just wanted to get faster, and I had a better chance of doing so there than with the generic running we were doing at school. Plyometrics, dot drills, weighted jumping, and resistance running were split across three days a week. It was strange that no one ever asked what those workouts looked like at the Center with my speed increasing significantly from my junior to senior year. It definitely worked.

The bell rang, but school letting out wasn't the end of the day. Our American Legion Coach, Mike Bromley, would meet us at the field or indoor to throw and hit for a few more hours. An amazing player in his time, Coach Bromley was a staple in the local baseball community. He always wore the same thing: thigh-high shorts, T-shirt, hiked-up white socks with a dark tan line, and a massive chew in his mouth. I had been working with him for three summers now and had improved each year. The previous offseason, we joined Abundant Life's then-baseball coach, Wes Johnson, and his team at the local batting cage to throw weighted balls and do specified band workouts to target the throwing motion. However, this offseason, the private school's coach had already moved on to the University of Central Arkansas. His move led to three of the 2A State Runner-Up players, D.J. Baxendale, Justin Treece, and Jake Chambers, transferring to Sylvan Hills. I played with Jake most of my life and knew Treece was but clueless when it came to D.J. The four of us, plus another transfer from Vilonia, Chris Perez, Ty, McKinney, and Dillon, were the usual takers on this extra practice time.

Transfers give Bears big boost.
Sometimes the rich just get richer.
Take Sylvan Hills. Already one of the state's best and most tradition-laden baseball programs, the Bears got an off-season boost they probably didn't need with the addition of three players from nearby Abundant Life.
All three players—shortstop [Justin] Treece, outfielder Jake Chambers and pitcher D.J. Baxendale—were key members of the Class 2A state runner-up Owls a season ago. But when then-Coach We Johnson left the Sherwood-based private school to take an assistant job with Central Arkansas, Treece, Chambers and Baxendale opted to make a move of their own.
"The only reason is because Wes Johnson left," Sylvan Hills Coach Denny Tipton said.[8]

The builders had already installed wooden boards on the side wall behind where the catchers would eventually set up for bullpen sessions. These became the backstops for our weighted ball workouts. Holes were drilled for weighted band clips right next to the boards. Every day, we had the same routine: stretch, use bands, throw weighted balls, throw regular baseballs, throw medicine ball drills, and then hit.

Coach Bromley had a brand-new computer program on his laptop. He filmed us hitting, uploaded it alongside a professional player with a similar swing, and compared every step of the swing. We could see our load, initial step, hand position, turn, barrel to the ball, follow-through, and everything in between. It was an absolute game-changer. None of us had seen anything like it. We spent hours hitting soft toss, working off the tee, batting practice on sunny days, and analysis on rainy days. There weren't any nets or mounds at the indoor facility yet. It didn't even have turf, just a concrete slab to take ground balls off on when it rained. We used every inch of the space.

Fall 2007 was also the offseason that I attached myself to former Sylvan Hills player Jeremy Brown. He was a 2002 graduate who was drafted out of high school by the New York Mets in the 43rd round. He chose to go to Pratt Community College in Kansas for a few years and was drafted again, this time in the 37th round by the Los Angeles Dodgers. He had come to a few of our workouts the previous year when Coach Johnson was around, but in 2007, I saw him almost every day. I used to watch him hit baseballs 350 ft off a tee behind home plate. Just a frozen rope before banging against the blue big wall in the outfield. His contact had a different sound. An echo caused by the wood bat that I had only heard watching the Arkansas Travelers at Ray Winder Field.

I played with some amazing baseball players through the years, some that would go on to the big leagues, but none quite to the point that Jeremy was in his baseball career. He and I traded places batting for an hour or so each day. Sometimes Perez or one of the others would stick around. Coach Bromley would yell at me to throw the ball harder to Jeremy, something he never said to my teammates. I felt like I was throwing full speed from forty feet away. It didn't matter. Jeremy was consistent. Everything he hit was pulled or up the middle. I thought he was going to break the L-screen. He showed me I still had a long way to go if I was ever going to make it to The Show. From 3:50 pm until dark almost every day, we were at the ballpark. I sacrificed a lot of time studying to stay at the field just that little bit longer. Always one more ball. One more round off the tee. One more look at my swing on the computer. Outside of church, there was no place I'd rather be.

2000 SHSO Orioles Baseball
Back Row: Coach Kevin Henard, Coach Doug Van Schoyck
Middle Row: Tristin, T.C., Devin, Ross, James, Robert
Front Row: Daniel T., Joshua, Jake, Daniel H., Ty

Friday, November 16, 2007
Sylvan Hills vs. Lake Hamilton Wolves
Semifinals of the Football State Tournament

Banners of blue and white hung from the cafeteria ceiling. Posters with players' names and numbers were falling off the walls. The Grizz Zone was long empty. Cars in the parking lot were still decorated with pawprints and phrases like *Beat Lake Hamilton* and *Let's Go Bears!* Reminders and remnants. That's all they were now. A football team with a brand new coach and a dream came up one game short. It was a contest based on the 0 - 4 start to the football season, dropping games against Catholic, Cabot, North Little Rock, and West Memphis, that Sylvan Hills should never have made it to in the first place.

"We missed out on some opportunities tonight," Sylvan Hills coach Jim Withrow said. "In a game like this, four or five plays can change the game for you, and it certainly did [for] us tonight. I'm proud of our guys, though. Coming out 0-4 to start the season, they could have folded it up and quit, but they fought hard all year and got themselves in the semifinals of the playoffs. Lake Hamilton is a great team, and you can't make mistakes against them if you want to give yourself

a chance."

  The Bears' amazing run finally came to an end Friday night at Wolf Stadium, as Lake Hamilton rolled off four first-half touchdowns on its way to a 44-16 win in the semifinal round of the 6A state playoffs.[5]

 Withrow's team couldn't keep up with the talented Lake Hamilton, despite their valiant effort. With the loss, Sylvan Hills' incredible season had come to an end.

  The Lake Hamilton Wolves won their twelfth game in a row to keep their perfect season intact. Sylvan Hills' QB Hunter Miller, FB Lawrence Hodges, and WR Mark Turpin did everything they could to bring home the win, but it just wasn't meant to be. Lake Hamilton would go on to lose against Texarkana in the championship game.

  I can only imagine the speech from Coach Withrow that night. A loss is a loss. That can be said for any sport. The feeling when it all comes crashing down doesn't smooth over well. The journey—growing up that's what we were told it's all about. From the first steps on the carpeted floor of Mom and Dad's house to the day that a child says goodbye for their senior year of school. It's not about what happens at the beginning or the end, but it's what is learned along the way. The pains and joys experienced on this journey are what are most important. Those are what grow us. What define us. We are told this in hopes that we won't give up, and that our experiences would lead us to become better men and women who will one day carry the next generation.

Try telling that to a locker room full of young men who just played their hearts out only to come up one win short. For many of those boys, they were done with football. This was their last game. Their last chance at glory. Seniors were on their way out. That's what made it difficult. Having it right there in your hand, making a miraculous streak come together at the end of the season, only to come up short against a tougher team. The players didn't want to hear about how well they did after the loss. They were angry and disappointed. Their journey wasn't worth it. The two- and three-a-days in the hot summer heat, the 6:00 am workouts before school, and the long sore nights after practice weren't worth coming up short.

For a school steeped in tradition and the expectation of winning, coming home without a championship was tough. The only bright spot for some of those seniors was that the loss to Lake Hamilton meant that baseball season was here. One more chance to bring home glory. But this story is not about the glory we hoped to achieve. This is not about individual ball players. It's not about winning and losing, or about rings and championships. This is a story of a team brought together by their journey.

CHAPTER 2

There were nine seniors on our 2008 baseball season. Jake Chambers transferred from Abundant Life after being part of several high-caliber teams. He had a cannon in right field and was also pitcher with a nasty knuckleball, though I don't think Coach ever let him throw it in a game. Chris Daulton was also an outfielder and pitcher. His fastball was difficult to catch up to when it was over the plate. J.T. Long was a standout catcher and resident jokester. A broken foot after football season set him back early in the season, but he recovered well. Hunter Miller became our number two starting pitcher and was arguably the best center fielder in the state. It was his gazelle-like speed and home run power that made him a complete player. Chris Perez was another excellent transfer, coming from Vilonia. His lefty arm and bat were unique among us, and his pitching would come in clutch throughout the season. Blake Rix was a fireball, played outfield, and had amazing speed on the basepaths. I had power from the right side, but at times, could be a strikeout liability. I worked at multiple infield positions over the years, but the hot corner was where I landed. Clint Thorton was probably the most consistent of all of us. He had played second base his entire life, had spotty power, but could always be counted on for a hit. Finally, Mark Turpin played shortstop and outfield. He had a great arm from deep in the hole, but his real passion was golf. It always took him a few weeks to get into his baseball swing.

All nine seniors started and lettered for one or more years at Sylvan Hills or another high school. Seven of us watched the 2005 Bears win State and felt the heartache of losing in the playoffs the next two years. Chambers knew that same feeling after losing in the 2A State Championship the year before. Between us, we had the right mix of infielders, outfielders, and pitchers to field every position on the diamond. With just us, we could have competed with half of the teams in our conference. In our ninth-grade year, we had our own team outside of the Varsity and JV squads. We played and beat multiple JV teams since most schools didn't have a ninth-grade team. Most of us had played together or against each other since we were five years old. It was nostalgic coming into the season knowing that we had come this far together. We couldn't have asked for better leadership for this year's team.

Technically, we weren't on the team yet. Coach made us try out every year, but I don't remember any stringent requirements like some other high schools in the area. In previous years, Coach brought on a couple of football players who had not played baseball before, but had something to offer, like energy or speed. Some of those guys would sit in the pressbox keeping track of the opponent's spray charts or trying to steal signs. Others would sit on a bucket just inside the dugout, tallying first-pitch strikes or keeping the pitch count. There were always a few who begged to be on the team or to be a manager, just to have a shot at winning a ring.

Saturday, May 14, 2005
Sylvan Hills vs. Jonesboro Golden Hurricanes
Finals of the Class 5A Baseball State Tournament

Tonight's game will mark the first time two teams from the AAAAA-East will meet for the state title. It's also the first state title game for Jonesboro and the first as a Class AAAAA member for Sylvan Hills, which won the Class AAAA title in 2003 and was runner-up a year ago.

"I think it's fun to have two teams out of

the East for a change," Ellis said. 'You always hear a lot of talk about teams from the West and from the Central and for good reason. You really always hear about teams from every conference but the East, so to have both us and Sylvan Hills in the final is really neat."

Jonesboro and Sylvan Hills split a conference doubleheader last month. The Bears, with ace Ashur Tolliver on the mount, beat Jonesboro and ace Jack McGrath 9-3 in the first game before the Hurricane came back and won 14-5 in the second game.

Sylvan Hills hasn't lost since that second game against Jonesboro, winning nine consecutive. Tolliver (8-1, 0.95 ERA) and McGrath (9-2, 2.11 ERA) will face off again tonight.

"We may have won that first game, [but] McGrath really dominated us," Tipton Said. "The first three innings we didn't even get on base. Brandon Eller hit a two-run home run in the fourth inning, and we were just able to get some more hits after that."

"I think you've got two quality pitchers and two quality teams with good hitters and it should be a good game. Early runs could be key," Ellis said. "If McGrath is on and throws well, he can be tough to score runs on, and I'm sure they think the same about Tolliver because he's a good thrower, too," Ellis said. "I think it'll be a fairly low-scoring

game, but you never know. I just know both of these teams are used to coming from behind and making things exciting. It should be fun."[9]

The lineup for the Sylvan Hills Bears:
#16 Jr Hayden Miller. Left Field. Avg .375
#24 Sr Chase Elder. Right Field. Avg .510
#27 Sr Brandon Eller. Short Stop. Avg .570
#25 Sr Matthew Presson. First base. Avg .450
#20 Jr Austin Gwatney. Center Field. Avg .355
#22 Jr Shawn Bybee. Second base. Avg .325
#3 Sr Kody Sanders. Designated Hitter. Avg .300
#13 Sr Dustin Baker. Catcher. Avg .265
#15 Sr Trey Enis. Third Base. Avg .260

Pitcher Jr Ashur Tolliver 8-1, 0.95 ERA
Head Coach Denny Tipton

The lineup for the Jonesboro Golden Hurricanes:
#1 Sr Derrick Coleman. Second base. Avg 375
#18 Jr Cody Pace. Center Field. Avg .342
#12 Sr Michael Johnson. Right Field. Avg .442
#23 Jr Murray Watts. First base. Avg .459
#7 Sr Hunter Smith. Third Base. Avg .486
#2 Sr Nic Culpepper. Designated Hitter. Avg .305
#42 Jr Eddy Price. Catcher. Avg .378
#3 Sr Jack McGrath. Pitcher. Avg .235
#13 Sr Justin Gambill. Left Field. Avg .298
#37 Jr Todd Ellis. Short Stop. Avg .400

Pitcher Senior Jack McGrath 9-2, 2.11 ERA
Head Coach Jim Ellis

TOP OF THE FIRST
Sylvan Hills

Miller flied out to center. Elder singled to left-center. Eller hit a two-run home run to deep right-field. Elder scored. Presson grounded out. Gwantney stuck out swinging.

2 runs, 2 hits, 0 errors, 0 left on base.

Sylvan Hills 2, Jonesboro 0

BOTTOM OF THE FIRST
Jonesboro

Coleman doubled to deep left-center. Pace tripled to deep right center. Coleman scored. Johnson singled. Pace scored. Watts singled up the middle, Johnson advanced to second. Smith bunted Johnson to third. Watts advanced to second. Culpepper hit a sacrifice fly to left field. Johnson scored. Passed ball by Baker, Watts advanced to third. Price struck out swinging.

3 runs, 4 hits, 0 errors, 1 left on base.

Sylvan Hills 2, Jonesboro 3

TOP OF THE SECOND
Sylvan Hills

Bybee flied out to center. Sanders reached on a walk. Baker singled down the right field line. Sanders advanced to second. Barnes pinch running for Sanders. Roark pinch running for Baker. Wild pitch by McGrath, advanced Barnes to [third], [Roark] to [second]. Enis sacrifice bunt scored Barnes. Roark advanced to third. Miller struck out looking.

1 run, 1 hit, 0 errors, 1 left on base.

Sylvan Hills 3, Jonesboro 3

TOP OF THE SIXTH

Sylvan Hills

Bybee reached on a walk. Taylor pinch hit for Sanders. Bybee advanced to second on a stolen base, took third on error by Price. Taylor grounded out to second. Bybee scored. Baker grounded out to second. Enis lined out to deep left field.

1 run, 0 hits, 1 error, 0 left on base.

Sylvan Hills 4, Jonesboro 3

BOTTOM OF THE SIXTH

Jonesboro

Watts homered to deep left field. Smith grounded out to second. Culpepper reached base on error. Price reached on fielder's choice. Culpepper forced out. Lee substituted to run for Price. Leed advanced on passed ball. McGrath reached on error. Lee advanced to third. Bennett substituted to run for McGrath. Gambill singled. Lee scored. Bennett advanced to second. Coleman grounded out to second.

2 runs, 2 hits, 2 errors, 2 left on base.

Sylvan Hills 4, Jonesboro 5

TOP OF THE SEVENTH

Sylvan Hills

Miller reached on error. Elder hit by pitch, Miller advanced to second. [Eller intentionally walked.] Presson singled to shallow right. Miller scored. Elder advanced to third, Eller advanced to second. Gwantney reached first on fielder's choice. Elder forced out, Eller advanced to third, Presson advanced to second. Eller scored on Bybee bunt. Presson advanced to third. Gwantney advanced to second. Passed ball scored Presson.

Gwatney advanced to third. Taylor singled to shallow left-center, Gwatney scored. Taylor stole second. Taylor advanced to third on passed ball. Baker flied out to shallow center.

4 runs, 2 hits, 1 error, 1 left on base.

Sylvan Hills 8, Jonesboro 5

Sylvan Hills	AB	R	H	RBI	Jonesboro	AB	R	H	RBI
Miller, lf	4	1	0	0	Coleman, 2b	4	1	1	0
Elder, rf	3	1	1	0	Pace, cf	3	1	1	1
Eller, ss	3	2	3	2	Johnson, rf	4	1	1	1
Presson, 1b	4	1	1	1	Watts, 1b	3	1	2	1
Gwatney, cf	3	1	0	0	Smith, 3b	3	0	0	0
Bybee, 2b	2	1	0	1	Culpepper, dh	2	0	0	1
Sanders, dh	1	0	0	0	Price, c	3	0	0	0
Baker, c	4	0	1	0	McGrath, p	3	0	1	0
Enis, 3b	1	0	0	1	Gambill, lf	3	0	1	1
Tolliver, p	0	0	0	0	Ellis, ss	0	0	0	0
Barnes, pr	0	1	0	0	Lee, pr	0	1	0	0
Taylor, ph	2	0	1	2	Bennett, pr	0	0	0	0
Roark, pr	0	0	0	0					
Dille, 3b	0	0	0	0					
TOTALS	27	8	7	7	TOTALS	28	5	7	5

Umpires - Schneider, Ray, Robber. **Time** - 2:00

Sylvan Hills	IP	H	R	ER	BB	SO
Tolliver	5	6	4	4	2	6
Eller **W**	2	1	1	0	0	1
Jonesboro	IP	H	R	ER	BB	SO
McGrath **L**	7	7	8	5	4	6

E - Tolliver, Dille, Bybee (2), Ellis, Price. **LOB** - Sylvan Hills 6, Jonesboro 6. **2B** - McGrath, Coleman. **3B** - Pace. **HR** - Eller, Watts. **SB** - Taylor, Bybee, Eller (2). **SH** - Enis, Bybee, Smith. **SF** - Culpepper.

Box Score	1	2	3	4	5	6	7	R	H	E
Sylvan Hills (25 - 8)	2	1	0	0	0	1	4	8	7	4
Jonesboro (25 - 8)	3	0	0	0	0	2	0	5	7	2

Denny Tipton is big on using the squeeze play, and it helped him and his Sylvan Hills Bears come up big with another state title.

The Sylvan Hills coach, known for winning big games by squeezing home runners, called a squeeze with one out in the top of the seventh inning Saturday night, and Shawn Bybee executed it to perfection.

Bybee laid down a soft bunt toward the third base line and Brandon Eller raced home for the go-ahead run to give Sylvan Hills the momentum on its way to an 8-5, come-from-behind victory over conference rival Jonesboro in the Class AAAAA State Championship Game at Baum Stadium.

Sylvan Hills (25 - 8) used a Jonesboro error, two stolen bases and a single from Matt Presson to tie the game at 5-5 before Eller scored on the squeeze to give the Bears a 6-5 lead.

"The squeeze seemed to really take some air out of Jonesboro," Tipton said.

So did a triple play in the second inning. With runners at first and second running on contact, pitcher Ashur Tolliver snagged Derrick Coleman's line drive and threw to Presson at first, who then relayed the ball to Eller at second to end the threat.

"The triple play was huge," Jonesboro Coach Jim Ellis said. "I felt like we were going to get us a run or two, maybe more. We had the opportunity to go ahead there and getting runs at that time would have been big."

But the Bears' second squeeze play of the game gave them the lead, and they scored two more runs in the inning on a passed ball and two hits to lead 8-5. Jonesboro went scoreless in its final at-bat as Sylvan Hills won the school's sixth state title, its second in the past three seasons and first as a member of Class AAAAA.

"We talked before the game that it could come down to a squeeze to win the game and you've got to be able to execute things like that," Tipton said. "Even though we were behind we knew we had a chance just like we have all year. We had our 1-2-3 hitters up, our best hitters all year long, and they came through for us."

And they did it in dramatic fashion for the second game in a row.

The Bears upset Bryant on Tuesday by scoring three runs with two out in the bottom of the seventh. While Saturday's runs were scored in the top of the final inning, they didn't lack dramatics.

Once again it seemed Sylvan Hills' luck was going to run out.

The Hurricane (25 - 8) used a leadoff home run from Murray Watts, a pair of errors and a single from Justin Gambil to score two runs in the sixth inning to take a 5-4 lead.

Sylvan Hills quickly got things going off Jonesboro starter and ace Jack McGrath in the seventh. Hayden Miller reached on an error, Chase Elder was hit by a pitch and Eller was intentionally walked. Presson singled home Miller to tie the game and an out later, Bybee's squeeze bunt gave the Bears the lead for good.

"[Tipton] likes to squeeze so it didn't surprise me one bit," Ellis said. "When you get in a situation with one out and a runner on third and people who can do it and there's not much you can do about it unless you're going to throw at the batter. There's not a whole lot of ways you're going to stop that. It got away from us after that."

Eller, who picked up a tournament victory against Rogers, pitched in relief against Bryant and was 3 for 3 Saturday night with a first-inning home run, was named tournament MVP after pitching the final two innings to pick up the victory.

"He's a gamer," Tipton said. "There's nobody else you want with the ball or at the plate in a key situation. He's the biggest clutch hitter I've ever had or the biggest clutch player to make a play or get an out."

Sylvan Hills, which was runner-up to Jonesboro in the AAAAA-EAST, scored two runs on two hits in the first inning, including a single from Elder and Eller's home run. Jonesboro, which was playing in the school's first title game, responded in their half with three runs on four hits off Tolliver.

The Hurricane took their first lead on a double from Coleman, a triple from Cody Pace and singles from Michael Johnson and Watts.

Sylvan Hills tied the game at 3-3 in the second as Trey Enis squeezed in a run, and it remained tied until the sixth when Bybee came through.

"We work on a lot of little things in practice knowing when it comes state tournament time something like that oculd be needed to win a game," Eller said. "We've worked on the squeeze a lot in practice. It came up big for us tonight."[10]

Upon entering baseball tryouts, our minds were consumed with thoughts of bringing home another title and wondering if there was a championship team among the tryouts. We reflected on our freshman season when the Bears won the 2005 5A State Championship, putting together a string of wins at the end of the season that defied all odds. Despite not winning the Conference that year, we managed to win Conference Titles in 2006 and 2007. But since that 2005 season, we struggled to get out of the second round of the tournament, with losses to Fayetteville High School in 2006 and West Memphis in 2007. Both of those Sylvan Hills teams had the same opportunities as the championship teams before them, but for them, it wasn't meant to be. However, for us, our determination was indescribable.

For the most part, there were no surprises in the tryouts. We already knew that Perez, D.J., Treece, and Chambers, though new to the school, would make the team. Coach also took eight or nine freshmen with decent talent, hoping to form a freshman team and fill in on the Junior Varsity. Among the freshmen, there was one standout in terms of speed. Mike Maddox was quiet,somewhat arrogant, and would get a few opportunities in the coming season.

A week after tryouts, Coach held our first team meeting in his classroom next to the gym, where we got to know the new players and discussed expectations for the year. Coach wanted to make it clear that bad behavior in the classroom would translate to less playing time. Outside of that, it was the usual lighthearted session. The new players, especially the freshmen, were always quiet and unsure of what they should be doing. There was a running joke that if any of the new freshmen had a girlfriend, he would have to break up with her to join the team. It was a joke, but Justin Jones didn't get the memo. This was the only year I remember someone actually going through with it. Obviously, the joke wasn't made clear enough, but it was amusing to watch the surprise on Coach's and the others' faces when Justin confirmed that he had indeed broken up with his girlfriend.

We picked up our uniforms before the night ended. The freshmen received a blue mesh jersey, which was old and extremely uncomfortable. The Varsity and Junior Varsity teams had blue, gray, white, and our favorite jerseys, black and blue. Everyone got white and gray pants for home and away games, respectively, a couple of pairs of blue socks, a blue belt, and white and blue fitted hats with that famous SH logo on them. Coach added a new hat this year, a blue crown with a black bill that looked great with the black jerseys. This year, we also got matching ball bags, which made the team look incredibly cohesive. Everything else had to be ordered by the player. Most of us already had letterman jackets, which were different from the ones the football team had and looked much better. Coach gave us the option of ordering matching windbreaker pullovers this year, which was a great idea since the February part of the season was always cold. We even went all out and got matching ear warmers. There wouldn't be a better-looking or more intimidating team out there this season.

I recall Treece approaching me that night after the meeting with either D.J. or Hunter, wanting to trade numbers with me. He desired his #1 for my #13, which apparently was his old number at Abundant Life. I informed him that he would have to wait until after I graduated if he still wanted it. I had worked hard to earn #13 for the past two years and was not willing to give it up my senior year. Some guys expressed their frustration with murmurs, believing that I would not be a starter, and Treece would be, so I should give him the number. I was infuriated. Whether or not I started, it did not matter. It was not about the number.

During my freshman year, when it was time to choose a number from the old blue, mesh jerseys, there were not many options. Jerseys had been replaced throughout the years, and the numbers were all over. Since very few freshmen ever traveled with the Varsity team, it did not matter if we had a duplicate number. My entire life, I had been #99, but that was not an option. This was time for a fresh start. When it was my turn to choose, I saw the #13. There was a senior that year, Dustin Baker, whom I had an art class with. He was a buff, goofy guy who played catcher and was #13. He would talk smack with a few of the other baseball players in the class, as well as with our art teacher, Mr. Green. Behind his desk, Mr. Green kept a full bucket of paint with a rope and handle attached to it. Dustin would regularly challenge Mr. Green to a forearm workout contest where they would alternate rolling the can up and down as many times as possible before the burn became too much. Based on the size of Mr. Green's forearms, he was never going to lose, but it was fun for all of us to watch.

Baker was a down-to-earth guy who was ready to graduate, but the most significant thing I recall about him was that he was kind. I got to know him well enough that he would stick up for me. Like at our first team practice of the Spring semester, which I did not know about. Because it had rained all day, it was a gym day. I quickly learned that it meant about three hours of running in the gym. Not knowing about practice, I did not have workout clothes and ended up running in jeans. I passed out on the concrete floor from being out of shape and not able to catch my breath. It was one of many laughable moments to come. Dustin watched a freshman nobody make a fool of himself, patted me on the back, and told me that it would get better. I would be okay. To keep my head up. Those words were enough, and he was right. It did get better after that first practice. So, there was no way I was giving up #13.

CHAPTER 3

Friday, January 25, 2008

A bitter cold had enveloped Arkansas. January was a mixed bag when it came to the weather. There had already been some snow the week before. While it wasn't enough to make a huge difference, snow was snow. Freezing rain and ice were normal a few times a year, but in the central part of the state, we didn't have the equipment to clear the roads like they do farther north. School had been canceled across some of the state including universities with high numbers of commuters but not everywhere.

The exact moment I found out escapes me. Somewhere around 8:40 in the morning. We didn't have texting at the time, so it was either through a phone call or on the news. But I remember the rush of emotions I felt. Confusion. Grief. Sadness. Anger. Pain. Literal pain as I thought about all the years I'd known my friend.

> *A wintry mix of ice and rain made for perilous roadways in Arkansas on Friday. Police said one man was killed early Friday in an accident stemming at least in part from the weather. Kyle Taylor Roark, 19, lost control of his truck, crossed the median and slamming into a tractor trailer. Roark was a freshman baseball player at Henderson State University and was on his way back to the school for a 9:00 am class. He had played baseball at Sylvan Hills High School in Sherwood last year.[11]*

> *Taylor Roark was a teammate, through and through. Roark called a freshman teammate at Henderson State about 8:40 a.m. Friday while driving from his home in Sherwood to Arkadelphia to make a 9 a.m. class . . . Shortly after Roark hung up the phone, he was killed when he hit a patch of ice on a bridge on Interstate 30, lost control of his truck, crossed the dividing line and hit a tractor-trailer near the Clark-Hot Spring county line, according to the Arkansas State Police.*

> *"He was talking to one of his teammates that was in the class with him right before the accident," Henderson State Coach John Harvey said. "Baseball is really about the last thing on*

our mind,' Harvey said. 'It takes something like this to show you how unimportant baseball is."

Roark was a three-year letterman and all-state selection at Sylvan Hills, hitting .430 with 41 runs, 33 walks, 22 stolen bases and 5 home runs his senior year in 2007. He was a member of the Bears' Class AAAAA state championship team as a sophomore in 2005. He also lettered three years in football, accumulating 600 yards on 40 receptions with 4 touchdowns his senior year, when he was a 6A-East all-conference selection.

"He was just a class act," Sylvan Hills baseball coach and assistant football coach Denny Tipton said. "Had him for four years in baseball. Also had him in football. He was a great young man. He always came to work. He would always pull pranks," Tipton said. "He was always trying to break the atmosphere. Taylor has been the most versatile player that I ever had," Tipton said. "He pitched, played shortstop, played outfield and then he had to catch his senior year. He played every position but first base." [60]

Taylor was a star. He wasn't supposed to be on the road. He had gone to Sherwood to spend time with his high school sweetheart, Hannah, and was making the trip back early for class. He didn't know if the class was already canceled or not due to the snow. Tragic doesn't come close to describing the situation. His life was cut short.

I can still picture Shod Neely yelling, *"Let's go, T-Cock!"*

from the dugout every time Taylor came up to bat. Roark. Number seven. T-Ro. T-Pain. Gaylord. *TTTTT!* All the goofy names we'd call him like Chipmunk because of the way he'd stuff his cheeks with food when Coach fed us on the long road trips. Taylor would laugh it off, sing some random song, or he'd bring the heat back on you. Whenever he and Garrett Eller were together, the team was never short of laughter.

TERRY J. DuBOSE, Little Rock
Schools needed to close.

If school officials were able to drive last Friday without problem, good for them. How many inexperienced drivers under the age of 20 were on the roads of Arkadelphia that morning? Between the high school and two colleges, I'm thinking that number would probably surprise us.

How sad that it took the death of a student for Henderson State University to close the campus Friday. Even sadder, it was the only school in Arkadelphia to do so.

Friday morning between 7 and 7:30, we received a hard sleet, and I fully expected that our public school district and both colleges would do the responsible thing: Close their campuses. Are they all so obsessed with making up one snow day that the safety of Arkadelphia students means so very little? Or do they need even a more dangerous situation than sleet and freezing temperatures to feel justified in closing school?

Obviously, they do. This leaves me wondering: What will it take for our school system to put the safety of our students and school staff before the schedules on its calendar? Unfortunately, the price to stay on schedule seems to be outrageously steep. I give my deepest sympathy to the family and friends of Taylor Roark. [12]

I remember our old morning announcement intro video where Taylor was seen stumbling down a flight of stairs with Daniel Powter's *"Bad Day"* playing in the background. The Teenage Mutant Ninja Turtles walk-up song when it was his turn to bat. I remember his perfect imitation of Coach Tipton running and the way he flexed to impersonate Coach Foor while yelling *"SWOLE!"* That was Roark's normal goofy self, doing whatever he could to make us laugh.

> *"The biggest thing I'll always remember about Taylor is him coming around the bases during the state title game with Bryant his sophomore year,"* Tipton said. *"That was the year Bryant was supposed to be unstoppable, and I can still see him coming around the bases for us to tie the game. I remember what a great leader he was for us. He was always a prankster, and he enjoyed the game so much."*
>
> *"It's been tough around here; he wasn't just a good athlete, he was class president his senior year, and he did great in the classroom,"* Tipton said. *"He had tons of friends, and everyone's trying to cope with it. We will honor him on the baseball team this season. We haven't decided exactly what we're going to do yet, but we will figure that out when things quiet down some."* [13]

But Taylor had a switch. He could turn his humor on and off whenever he wanted. I vividly remember his senior year in 2007 when I was spotting him on the bench press. He was struggling with the very last rep and was determined to push every ounce of energy out of his arms before asking for help. His face was already turning red. When I tried to grab the bar to rack the weight, he snapped at me. *"No. Don't touch it."* He wanted to complete the set even though the weight was too much. Taylor was a perfectionist, and it reflected in everything he did, from hitting BP to stepping out of the cage after saying *"Just one more"* at least twenty times. Taylor's leadership and example over the years were instrumental to the team's success.

Two things are pretty much certain every baseball season at Sylvan Hills: The Bears are going to win the conference championship, and at least one player will sign on with a college to play baseball. Both of those happened again this year as Sylvan Hills took the 6A East title and senior catcher Taylor Roark signed a national letter of

intent to play baseball for the Henderson State University Reddies in Arkadelphia.

Roark is a rare athlete capable of playing anywhere on the field. He became Sylvan Hills' catcher out of necessity, but has the speed and arm to play centerfield. Roark was also a pitcher for the Bears. The senior Bear's versatility is one advantage that could help him see playing time early on as a Reddie. Henderson will be bringing in several new players this season. One Reddie who will still be on campus will provide a familiar face for Roark. Former Sylvan Hills Bear Cody Duncan is currently a sophomore at Henderson. Duncan hit .270 for the Reddies this past season and led the team with a .432 on base percentage.

Henderson State didn't have the best season this year, finishing 20-36, but the team did win seven of its last 10 games to post a positive note leading into Roark's first season on the campus. Roark excels in more than baseball. The senior was also a starter for the football team at wide receiver and has a 3.6 GPA in the classroom, and scored a 27 on his ACT.[14]

His stats were solid through and through — including a batting average of over .450 his senior year — but none was more impressive than his on-base average of .708. He also took part in the Xtra Innings Classic at UALR as a junior. He was on the 5A state champion Bears team in 2005 as a sophomore as starting catcher.[13]

I spoke with Coach Tipton at some point, but it's all a blur. I don't even recall going to school the following days, though I know I did. Practice was canceled, but the team still met to discuss what had happened and what the future held. It was not easy. The team was in shock, devastated, and unable to comprehend the loss.

The funeral hit us hard. That night, my parents and I drove to the funeral home. There was no parking, and the line stretched out the door and down the street. Inside, it was standing room only. We waited for hours, seeing old friends we hadn't seen in ages, classmates, and recent graduates. People had come from all over the state. Dad and others told stories, struggling to come to terms with the tragedy. I just listened. I didn't have the words. Coach, the team, family, and friends were all there.

Finally, we made it to the front, and I couldn't hold back the tears any longer. There were pictures, jerseys, and signed baseballs. Taylor's mom, Lisa, was there, and I gave her a big hug. She told me to grab a marker. I looked at the casket, a plain wooden box, simple, for the unexpected. Written all over it were notes of prayers and hope, messages of love telling him how much he meant to us, how much we missed him, and how we'd see him again someday. We would take care of things while he was gone.

Taylor Kyle Roark, age 18, of Shewood, passed away Friday, January 25, 2008 as a result of a traffic accident. He was born July 19, 1989, in Little Rock. Taylor graduated in 2007, as an Honor Graduate and class president from Sylvan Hills High School. He was currently attending Henderson State University on a

baseball scholarship. Taylor was a memeber of Faith Baptist Church of North Little Rock.[15]

These are just a few of the hundreds of messages left for Taylor after he passed:

"Mrs. Lisa and Mr. Kelly. I know it has been several years now, but I still remember our trip to St.Louis and Taylor's first Cardinal game. We all had a blast and I'm so glad [y'all] came with us. I'm honestly blessed to have talked to Taylor about 2 months ago on the internet. We lost touch after the Indians, but it was really good catching up with him and talking about old times. I have vivid memories of Taylor stroking that ball all over Billy Mitchell field. At first he was shy and distant, but after he warmed up, man he would make us laugh so hard. He was an awesome guy and I'm blessed to have known him and have him as a friend. I like to think that Jesus has got Taylor batting in the 4 hole up there in heaven to knock in a few runs. My thoughts and prayers are with you and your entire family. You raised an amazing son and he will be missed." - Zack Taylor, Ruston LA. Former teammate.

"Taylor [we've] been together for a long time and we played football together for a while to. Taylor [I'm] at hinds community college running track, just now everytime [I] long jump [I'll] be thinking about you. LOVE YOU MAN"

- Jeff Henderson, North Little Rock, AR. Former teammate.

"Lisa and Kelly, we are so sorry to hear of the loss of Taylor. Such an exceptional young man who will be missed by all who had the privilege of knowing him. Our thoughts and prayers are with your family and Hannah during this time." - The Gwatney Family. Family friends.

"To the Roark family: I am saddened by your loss. Taylor was a bright spot in my AP class, and he will be missed." - Kathryn Young, NLR, AR. High School Teacher.

"To Lisa, Kelly, and family, my thoughts and prayers are with you during this time. And to Taylor, my house will not be as bright knowing you won't come [through] my front door with Andrew, Garrett, Tyler, and the gang. I'll truly miss your patented 'MR. Bir' greeting. I'll miss our arguements about the Cardinals and Marlins and the Hogs and Hoosiers. Kenny and Barry are better guys because of you. But as long as I can watch 'Meet The Parents,' I'll always remember you Gaylord." - Tim Bir, NLR, AR. Family friend and umpire.

"Mr. and Mrs. Roark: I am truly sorry for your loss. I can only imagine your pain. Taylor was such an exceptional young man. He was one

of the kind of kid that keeps me in coaching. Always in a good mood with a smile on his face, willing to [do] anything and everything to help. Something very important to me that I will always remember about Taylor is how nice he was to my son and how much he always took the time to 'play around' with Reid. Reid and I both looked up to him a great deal." - Coach Fawcett, Sherwood, AR, High School Coach.[15]

Our former baseball announcer and long-time friend, Andrew Reynolds, wrote a flawless poem in honor of Roark, which was published in our 2008 Sylvan Hills yearbook, paying homage to his personality and memory.

Reminiscence in Remembrance
by: Andrew Reynolds

On 25 all of these mixed emotions,
Eight months to the day of your signed promotion.
You left us behind to pick up where you left it,
Your early departure was least expected.

Your legacy is true, your diamond skills too,
In all the right ways, representing white and blue.
For years I called SS number seven,
As I'm sure you've made Harry Carey do in heaven.
Made the switch to backstop, unselfish it seemed,
Then walked to the plate to the TMNT theme.
The park will surely miss those timely ole' quirks,
And your face in the dugout with those big goofy smirks.
Rochester 2 days, Denver and Sherwood,

"Cincy" you'd say; followed by "Man, I'm good."
Coach T wanted to learn it and wished that he could,
"Tell me!" he'd say but stubbornly you never would.
"Bowed" you'd scream in the direction of Coach Foor.
But once workouts were through he'd have to help you off the floor.
On your finger sat a ring commemorating '05,
An achievement we'll remember as long as we're alive.
A Reddie you became with foam finger in hand,
I still remember the day, "Take a pic of me man!"
The diamond will miss you, and vice versa it goes,
But you left your mark, and the whole world knows.

Those age-old battles, the Hogs and West V.
You know I was better, you never even beat me!
Give me one more game and I'd probably let you hang,
Pat White goes 80, you say "I got this, man."
Kelly called me a cheater for the simis in '02.
And I gotta admit, man, I think I fouled you.

Gary Ervin was the worst, Dontell Jefferson, too,
Turnovers galore would always aggravate you.
"You can't spell 'suck' without USC"
"Was that 70-17? Are you kidding me?"
You never got to come up and kick in the 'ville.'
But the open invitation is wide open, still.

I've begun to scratch the surface and had a little fun,
But recounting every memory just cannot be done.
Too many to count but I remember a few,
A lot of them involve that girl Hannah and you.
Coldstone with Shelbs and your new fly gear,

Eating my cookies that had been sitting a year.
I was always envious of the bond you two shared,
Even during a fight you could show that you cared.

Taylor Kyle Roark, you now eat bread unleavened
With the big guy upstairs in a place called heaven
Look in from time to time; our sorrows you will leaven,
May the Lord forever bless our lucky number seven.[16]

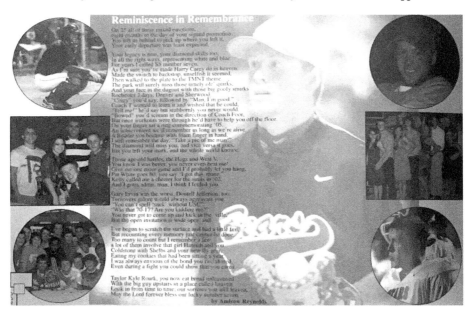

We did everything we could to honor and remember Taylor. TR7. Taylor Roark #7. We plastered his name and number on everything imaginable: wristbands, headbands, batting gloves, hats, and patches. Coach even hung a banner from the big blue wall out in left field. During the seventh inning of every game, we'd rush out and pound it. For the rest of the season, we retired his number, and Henderson State hung his jersey in the outfield as a tribute.

Even though we tried our best to commemorate Taylor's memory, there wasn't much time to process the tragedy before life resumed its normal pace. Despite our grief, we had to keep moving forward. That season, we played every game in honor of Taylor, our teammate, and our friend, our brother.

CHAPTER 4

Friday, February 1, 2008

Our first game was scheduled for February 19th, opening the season against Catholic, but we weren't prepared. The Blue and White game exposed that, and the freezing cold weather had a huge impact on us. The snow kept coming, and when it wasn't snowing, torrential downpours cancelled our home tournament. In the past, Coach would call in some help from the local hospital or news station to have a helicopter land on the field to dry it out, but that moment never came. Even if it had, it would probably have rained the next day.

Our only refuge was our new indoor facility, which was coming together but still not complete. We spent several days hauling in six-foot-tall rolls of old turf from War Memorial

Stadium. What a workout! A few of us would get the turf lined up and roll it out to the next edge, while others were set up with box knives or wide strips of tape. We'd get it rolled out and cut, then spin it around to repeat the process. The center section was simple, but the edges took a bit longer because they had to wrap around the irregular frame of the building. Then we worked on getting the edges together so there wasn't any concrete showing between the stripes. The leftover scraps were cut as hitting mats to keep from wearing holes in the floor. It was amazing the difference the turf made compared to the concrete floor we had practiced on the whole fall.

But the facility didn't pay for itself. After years of local business donations, students starting and then graduating without seeing it complete, this was the year. It had to be the year. The city picked up part of the bill. Our Annual Hit-A-Thon raised some funds, although it was postponed several times due to wet conditions. Businesses and parents donated. We even gave local kids a chance to learn through several skills clinics, something that the American Legion team generally did during the summer but was needed now.

> *The Sylvan Hills Bears and head coach Denny Tipton will be hosting a series of baseball skills clinics in February. All money earned by the clinics will go toward the new indoor baseball facility. There will be a hitting clinic on February 9-10. A pitching clinic on February 16-17 and a defensive clinic on February 23-24. Clinics on individual days will also be offered on February 5, 7 and 12. The clinics are for baseball players*

age 7-15. The fee for one clinic is $60 with
a $10 discount for each additional clinic. Call
the Sylvan Hills fieldhouse for more information.
The Sylvan Hills Bears have won multiple state
championships.[17]

Perhaps it was the combination of excitement over the new facility, anxiety about bad weather, the extensive fundraising efforts we were undertaking, or the lack of intensive running practices like in previous years, but this season felt far from ordinary. Adding to the oddness was the Optimist Club cleaning out their food and beverage storage to discover that all of their Gatorade and 2-liter drinks were past their expiration date. Rather than discard them, they generously offered them to us for free. It seemed a bit peculiar at first, but we didn't think too much about it. We carried case after case down to the field storage and even more to the indoor facility. It's almost comical to think that we lacked working restrooms and running water at the indoor facility, yet we had a mini-fridge fully stocked with Gatorade. Now, all that remained was for Coach to finalize the depth chart and kick off the season.

We had a team full of talented players. Depth was not an issue. Every position had a capable backup, and fortunately, we had no more injuries to deal with. The outfield was particularly strong with great arms and speed. The infield was close to being set as well, although Nathan and I competed in several practices, taking grounders and dodging Coach Foor's flying fungos to secure a starting position. We often stayed until sunset, or when Coach was too tired to continue, only then did we finally head to the indoor.

Sylvan Hills High School Baseball Varsity Roster

#	Name	Position	Height	Weight
1	Justin Treece	INF	5'7"	155 lbs
2	Tyler Van Schoyck	C	5'11"	155 lbs
3	Mark Turpin	INF/OF	6'0"	180 lbs
5	Blake Hannon	INF	5'9"	155 lbs
5	Michael Maddox	OF	5'8"	145 lbs
6	Jordan Griffin	OF	5'8"	150 lbs
8	D.J. Baxendale	P	6'1"	175 lbs
9	Michael Lock	INF	5'11"	170 lbs
11	Casey Cerrato	INF/OF	5'9"	150 lbs
12	Taylor Pennington	C/INF	6'3"	195 lbs
13	T.C. Squires	INF	6'0"	190 lbs
14	Jake Chambers	P/OF	5'9"	190 lbs
15	J.T. Long	C	5'10"	220 lbs
16	Korey Arnold	INF/OF	5'10"	165 lbs
17	Ryan Dillon	INF	5'8"	145 lbs
18	Jordan Spears	INF/P	6'3"	185 lbs
19	Blake Evans	INF	6'1"	170 lbs
21	Chris Perez	INF/P	6'0"	185 lbs
22	Blake Rix	OF	5'8"	175 lbs
23	Justin Jones	OF	5'9"	150 lbs
24	Hunter Miller	P/OF	6'0"	185 lbs
25	Chris Daulton	P/OF	5'11"	180 lbs
26	Jordan Bland	OF	5'10"	165 lbs
27	Nathan Eller	INF/P	5'10"	165 lbs
28	Clint Thorton	INF	5'7"	175 lbs
33	Eric McKinney	INF	5'10"	150 lbs

Depth Chart

Catcher

1. J.T. Long
2. Ty Van Schoyck
3. Jordan Spears

First Base

1. Blake Evans
2. Chris Perez
3. Taylor Pennington

Second Base

1. Clint Thorton
2. Eric McKinney
3. Ryan Dillon

Third Base

1. T.C. Squires
2. Nathan Eller
3. Michael Lock

Shortstop

1. Justin Treece
2. Mark Turpin
3. Korey Arnold

Outfield

1. Hunter Miller
2. Jake Chambers
3. Chris Daulton
4. Blake Rix
5. Casey Cerrato
6. Justin Jones

7. Michael Maddox

Pitching

1. D.J. Baxendale
2. Hunter Miller
3. Jordan Spears
4. Chris Perez
5. Jake Chambers
6. Blake Evans
7. Chris Daulton
8. Nathan Eller

Tipton became more hands-on in the cage during our batting practice sessions. He threw ten pitches to each player, humming the ball from forty feet away. There was no time to think, only react. We had to be ready for the ball and hit it where it was pitched.

In the past, I had a tendency to dwell on my misfortunes rather than my successes, which affected my confidence. No matter how many times Coach told me to "*Shake it off*" or how good my Dad's coaching from the stands was, I couldn't help overanalyzing every situation to the point where I became a liability to myself and the team. Comments from Coach Tipton like "*I wish Hunter had your work ethic*" were meant to compliment my effort, but I took them as a slight. I knew Hunter was more talented than I was, but it hurt to be compared to him like that.

Hunter and I didn't get along. Every season, he came up with a new nickname for me, which often caused issues with other teammates. In my sophomore year, he called me "*Shin guards*" because I was a backup catcher. I tried to play it off by wearing them everywhere, even to class and in restaurants. Junior year, he called me *"Grandpa"* and *"Cankles"* because of the size of my calves. I grew tired of this nickname the most. He knew it bothered me, but he didn't care. During one practice our senior year, I finally confronted him about it and told him off. I didn't need to be his friend, but I needed him to respect me and my skills. Nothing changed that day, and he even gave me a new nickname, *"Angry."* But I didn't care. If being Angry was what it took to get him to leave me alone, then so be it.

This off-season was going to be different for me. In fact, as we approached our first game against Catholic, I felt more confident than ever before. Working out with D.J. and utilizing Coach Bromley's new technology during the off-season had me feeling incredible. I had taken countless ground balls at third base, swung tens of thousands of times over the last few months, and spent hours at the running clinic. All of this had boosted my confidence, and I was now gunning for the starting role at third base, instead of the DH role I had played during the previous season. I had also crushed base hits off of D.J., Spears, and Chambers during our pre-season scrimmages. The heavy rains during the Spring had flooded the infield, but we adapted by setting up bases in left field.

During one practice, Coach brought in two new bats, red Louisville Slugger TPX EXOs, one 33/30 and a 32/29. Coach instructed us to try them out, perhaps because he could get a deal on them or the Louisville Slugger rep was looking for a new customer. Spears was pitching for this scrimmage, and I grabbed the 33/30 and stepped into the box. I don't remember the count, but I do remember that Jordan was throwing gas. I swung through at least one pitch, probably a fastball. At that time, Spears only threw a fastball and curve. His 6'3" frame put him closer to the plate when he pushed off the rubber.

My approach was simple: see ball, hit ball, foul off anything close, make solid contact, and put the ball in play. Jordan left one up in the zone and a little inside, and I crushed it over the big blue wall in left field. It was a no-doubter. I took off toward first base, intending to turn off the field to head back to the dugout to grab my glove, but Coach yelled at me to take my jog around the bases. Whether it was because he had never seen me hit a homer in person or because he wanted Jordan to feel the full weight of missing his spot, I went ahead and jogged the bases. I picked up the new EXO and handed it off to the next batter with a quick *"I like this new bat, Coach."* The swing put a dent in the barrel, too. Talk about boosted confidence. In my mind, this was the moment that sealed the deal for me in grabbing the starting spot at third base.

Tuesday, February 19, 2008
Sylvan Hills @ Catholic Rockets
Non-Conference Opponent

At 2:15 pm, I informed Mrs. Harris I was leaving, having already given her a note and reminded her that it was game day. Shortly after, an office aide made an announcement over the intercom, releasing the baseball team. I grabbed my backpack and headed out to the parking lot, where the team jumped into their trucks. During our last practice, Coach had instructed us to meet at the indoor, which was a departure from our usual meeting spot at the football fieldhouse or down at the field.

As we arrived at the facility, Mr. B was already there, waiting for us in the bus. Mr. Blackwood was a devoted supporter of our team and never missed a game, whether he was cheering us on at home or accompanying us on road trips. For every two to three-hour trip to West Memphis or Mountain Home, he was there. Mr. B's loyalty extended beyond just the baseball team; he had been attending Sylvan Hills football and basketball games since the 1960s and had been following the baseball program since 1971. He was a program staple, and we couldn't start a game until he delivered that brown paper sack filled to the brim with bubble gum.

Bill was very well known, and loved, by so many athletes, students, teachers, coaches, parents, sports fans, and members of the community, early on he became known most affectionately as "Mr. B." His many years of dedication to Sylvan Hills brought about the honor of having the football stadium named after him. Thanks to Coach Denny Tipton and the group who helped make that possible. Being the humble man he was and while feeling immense gratitude, Bill never quite grasped just how much he was appreciated.[19]

We parked our vehicles, got dressed in the parking lot, loaded up the team equipment, and jumped aboard. I grabbed my portable anti-skip CD player with The Art of Translation by GRITS already ready to play.

The first game of the season was against the purple and gold Catholic High School Rockets at historic Lamar Porter Field, a former semi-pro baseball field built in the 1930s. It was the perfect venue to start the season. Both teams warmed up on the field, and the Rockets paid respects in the wake of Taylor's passing. The national anthem played, and those famous words were said, *"Let's play ball!"*

After a bad top of the first inning, we took the field, and I got that first start of the season at third base. The first contact of the game for Catholic was a ball hit right at me. I was playing even with the bag, watching for a bunt, and got a hard ground ball instead. The sandy grass. The crushed red-brick infield dirt. The ball stayed low, and there was no bounce. It went right through my legs, E5. It couldn't have started any worse for me. Thoughts poured in. How did I screw this up? I didn't stay down on the ball. Didn't watch it all the way into the glove. Tried to throw before fielding it. My confidence dropped.

The second batter steps in. *Ding.* Another ground ball right at me. I was playing up on the grass this time, which I hated, expecting a bunt to move the runner over. Instead, I got another quick shot, glove side. This time, I started the first leg of the 5-4-3 double play, correcting my mistake from the previous play. Redemption. Two down. I moved past the error, and we finished the inning scoreless and went back to the plate.

I don't remember much except that one of my first at-bats of the season was a battle. I quickly got two strikes, and I could see Coach rethinking his decision to start me from the third base box. He would put his hands on his head and face the outfield for the first few seconds after each pitch and me stepping out of the box to get the sign. There weren't any signs to give. I just had to hit the ball. I fought back to a 3-2 count, fouled off three or four pitches, and fought hard. My confidence was heading back up again. This rollercoaster of trying to show I deserved this spot while blocking out the whispers from the stands and dugout was tough. I hated the feeling. It either ended in a walk or a strikeout. No solid contact.

In a different at-bat, the bad beats picked up again. I fouled a ball off my foot that rolled down toward third base in foul territory. Somehow, it spun fair. I stayed in the box, knowing it hit off my foot, but the umpire didn't call it foul. The ball was thrown to first, and I was out. Seriously. How could he not see it hit off my foot? I screamed at him from the field the next inning when one of Catholic's players fouled a ball off his foot and immediately got the call. It was ridiculous. It hurt, but I couldn't control the umpires. I finished the game 0 for 2 with a walk, a strikeout, and a missed call. Not great. As a team, we struggled, losing our first game of the season to Catholic by a score of 1-2. It was not the start that we wanted or were expecting.

Thursday, February, 28, 2008
Sylvan Hills vs Bryant Hornets
Pather Invitional Tournament

The struggles didn't stop there. After wins against Central and Sheridan, we lost to Bryant in the Panther Invitational Tournament. That one hurt. We didn't get our first hit of the game until the fifth inning. We were down 1-4. Clint singled into left and stole second, and then Spears walked. A couple of groundouts followed, and Clint was able to score, making it 2-4. Hunter hit a shot to the shortstop, which was booted, scoring another run and making it 3-4. A pitching change was followed by Hunter stealing second, and a wild throw to second allowed him to get to third. Then, D.J. walked, and Ty pinch-ran for him. So we had runners on first and third with me in the six-hole batting. Ball one. The second pitch was close, a check swing, but called a ball. Ty stole second base without a throw, which upset Bryant's coach. He wanted an appeal on the check swing, but it wasn't granted, and an argument started. Time was called, and their coach visited the mound to talk over the second and third situation, but really, he just wanted another chance to yell at the umpire. When play started up again, I was sitting 2-0, looking for a fastball middle-in to drive, and I got it. I turned on the pitch down the third baseline. It should have been a two-run double, putting us ahead 5-4, but it wasn't.

"Foul ball!" the home plate umpire yelled as I rounded first. Coach Tipton at third couldn't believe the call. No one could. The stands were in an uproar. Now, our coach was arguing with the umpire. It was another bad break for me. A stolen hit and our lead wiped. I made it back into the box and drew a walk to load the bases. Another pitching change led to a hard ground ball to third base, which was booted for another error in the inning, allowing Hunter to score. We were all tied up at 4-4. Jake grounded into an infielder's glove up the middle, but the runner beat the throw, sliding safely into second, scoring Ty, and taking the lead 5-4. That ended up being our second and last hit of the game, which was crazy. The lineup turned over, and Clint was back up to bat. He hit a swinging bunt that dribbled down to third. I took off running toward home and slid in as Kaleb Jobe caught the ball for the force play and third out of the inning,

except the umpire ruled that Jobe's foot was off the bag. I was safe, making it 6-4, and we were ahead. Another argument from their coach followed by a groundout by Spears ended the top of the fifth inning, bases still loaded. It was a crazy inning, to say the least.

Bryant tied the game in the bottom of the inning, 6-6, and then it became a pitching duel. There was nothing for us in the sixth or seventh innings. Jake led off with a walk in the eighth. As he tried stealing second, Clint interfered with the catcher. He became out one, and Jake had to go back to first. Perez pinch-hit for Spears. Treece was up next. Both flew out to centerfield, and there were no runs in the eighth. Hunter was pitching and got the first out easy, but then he gave up back-to-back singles and hit the next batter, loading the bases. Hunter induced a double-play ball to second base, but it was bobbled, flipped to Treece at second for an out, but the relay to first wasn't in time. Bryant scored on the walk-off fielder's choice in the eighth. It was a tough loss against a good team, but we picked up our gear and moved forward.[61]

We went on to beat non-conference opponents, the Cabot Panthers 8-0 and Beebe Badgers 14-2 in the Jacksonville Tournament. However, we followed it up with a loss to our closest conference rival, the Jacksonville Red Devils, in the championship game. It was another tough game. They even doused their coach in a Gatorade bath after beating us. It felt like they were practicing for the State Championship. The loss hit deep. Coach used that moment as a regular reminder of how other teams felt about beating the Sylvan Hills Bears.

Our team was dominant but inconsistent. Treece broke his hand in the Jacksonville tournament, which set us back. We either smoked the other team or engaged in an all-out battle over a couple of runs. Three of our first four losses were by one run. Those were the games where our offense struggled. We couldn't string enough hits together. However, when we did get on base, we were a fast team. Coach wasn't afraid to play small ball, steal bases, sacrifice bunt, or call for a hit and run. Almost every baserunner had a chance at taking an extra base. We had seven stolen bases in the Bryant game alone. But it wasn't always enough. Good teams find a way to win, and we were playing some really good teams early on. It didn't help that we were the favorites to win the 6A East Conference, and every team was throwing their best pitchers at us.

Tuesday, March, 11, 2008
Sylvan Hills @ North Little Rock Charging Wildcats
Non-Conference Opponent

The rivalry game against North Little Rock was a nail-biter. We had a game plan and stuck to it throughout the game. We even ran the Lollipop play, which really amped up the team. NLR had one extremely fast player, and the scouting report showed that if he got on base, he was going to steal—100% chance. Lollipop was a trick play to confuse the runner and tag him for an out. Basically, on the steal, the pitcher throws a normal pitch outside the zone to the hitter. The catcher throws a short popup to the second baseman as if the batter hit a fly ball. Everyone else's job is to convince the runner to stop running to second or to leave second base completely to go back to first for the easy tag. We'd practiced it as part of our bunt drills every day for years, but we'd never had a surefire chance to use it. Until this game.

Early in the game, our target got on first. Pick off. Safe. Pick off. Safe. His lead never changed. We knew he was going. Coach Tipton called the play. I could hear the whispers from the bench—they were part of this too. I was playing the grass in case of a bunt, but the pitch should be plenty out of the zone to avoid it. My job was to yell and cover third should the runner round second. The pitcher got set. He lifted his leg, and the runner was off. The catcher shot a short fly ball to second, and the whole dugout yelled, "*Up!*" Turpin was covering second base and was pointing to the sky as the runner approached him. He slid in but got confused when he saw Clint with the ball. Immediately, he jumped to his feet and turned back toward first. An easy throw to first, and the tag applied for the out. We got him. The play worked to perfection. NLR's coach was stunned at third base. He couldn't believe what happened. We almost couldn't believe it either.

Trick plays over the years had been hit-or-miss. The double-squeeze play with Nathan Van Schyock running from second base and cutting through the infield in front of third base to score two runs worked to perfection. The next year, Conway saw right through Nathan Eller's bee play as he screamed and swatted at imaginary bees in the infield. That one gave all of us a good laugh. Lollipop's success was another badge of honor, but once other teams know about it, it's burned. We wouldn't be able to use it again this season. We were glad it worked. The excitement was short-lived as our bats struggled again, plating only a few in the 3-4 loss. I had a chance at third to make a tough play charging a slow roller to send us to another inning, but I ran out of time. The runner was safe on first, and he worked his way around on a couple of hits to score. It sucked. We were 4-4 on the season to this point, with conference games right around the corner.

I felt my confidence waning again, but I shouldn't have. The competition was stiff. Central, Bryant, Cabot, and NLR were in the class above us. These were larger schools, had their own districts and funds, and had a deeper funnel for talent in their respective areas. Sylvan Hills High School was part of the PCSSD, which incorporated a wide area and multiple high schools. Excuses. That's all.

During our ninth game of the season, which was a home game against Jacksonville, I finally felt like I had settled into my role on the field and in the box. I managed to get a hold of a fastball early in the game and launched it off the left-center wall, around 340-350 ft, resulting in a double. It's the only thing I recall from that game, apart from my disappointment in not hitting it over.

Earlier in the season, Coach bought a camera to record our at-bats. During the offseason, sitting with Coach Bromley and comparing swings had made a difference for me, and I'm sure Coach Tipton thought the same would be helpful for everyone. At the first practice after a game, players were given the opportunity to watch our at-bats. However, the camera was clunky, with a small screen and a view that was twenty or more feet away. All the clips were split up based on time, rather than a player's AB. This made it challenging to navigate. When I finally had my chance to watch, I immediately searched for that first hit to see what I did right. It was a pretty swing, but the launch angle was low, which resulted in a double instead of a home run.

As I moved through the sequence, trying to find my next at-bat, Coach Foor must have thought I was taking too long, or he already knew something that I hadn't been informed of, because he yelled at me to get back to hitting. I wasn't sure if it was someone else's turn or not. I couldn't have had the camera for more than a few minutes, and I wasn't finished checking my at-bats, so I told him that I wasn't done yet. He didn't like my response, but I didn't care. I was searching for feedback on my swing that I wasn't receiving elsewhere, and this was the most concrete way for me to see what I was doing without Bromley's program. I needed more time. Coach Foor yelled back several times before finally coming over and taking the camera from me. I was angry and walked off to the other side of the indoor to cool down.

Friday, March 14, 2008

Sylvan Hills has boasted a strong baseball program for decades, with state titles in 1965, 1974, 1978, 1981, 2003, and most recently in 2005. I had the privilege of playing with many of the players from that 2005 team who were now taking on college ball. In early March, the Sherwood Voice newspaper ran a player update on recent graduates from the Sherwood area, serving as a great reminder right before conference play of what we had to look forward to right.

Sherwood has been a haven for baseball players for years, with several area players continuing their careers through the college ranks.

Arkansas State
Brandon Eller (Sylvan Hills) is a little down so far this year with a .224 average as of Monday, but he does lead the Indians in doubles, is third in RBIs, fourth in hits and third in assists on defense.

UALR
Ashur Tolliver (Sylvan Hills) hasn't had many starts on the mound in the young season and is 0-1 with 14 strikeouts in 13 innings.

Freshman Ross Bogard (Sylvan Hills) has seen limited time this year.

Arkansas Tech

Austin Gwatney (Sylvan Hills) is having a solid season as a starter for the Wonder Boys this year. Gwatney is currently hitting .267 and is 5 of 5 stealing bases.

Chase Elder (Sylvan Hills) has come off the bench for the Wonder Boys for two hits this year, both doubles.

Nathan Van Schoyck (Sylvan Hills) has seen limited time so far this season.

UCA

Kent Taylor (Sylvan Hills) is fourth for the Bears this season with a .320 average and is also fourth on the team in RBIs.

Payton Seelinger's (Abundant Life) average is down right now at .224, but he is second on the Bears in runs and home runs.

Henderson State

Cody Duncan (Sylvan Hills) has come back from injury and is batting an even .400. He doesn't have quite as many at bats as the rest of the starters, but has been hot this season. Duncan also has a .633 slugging percentage and a .561 on base percentage.

Limited information could be found on

Zac Ray (Abundant Life) at Louisiana State
University at Shreveport and Jarrett Boles (Sylvan
Hills) at Pratt Community College.[19]

In addition to the success of Sylvan Hills collegiate baseball players, Arkansas as a whole had plenty of talent working their way into the Big League.[10]

Minor League Position Players

PLAYER	COLLEGE/HOMETOWN	POS	TEAM (CLASS-ORG)	AVG	G	AB	R	H	2B	3B	HR	RBI	SB
Jason Belcher	Walnut Ridge	LF	Harrisburg (AA-Washington)	.185	8	27	2	5	1	0	1	4	0
Cody Clark	Fayetteville	C	Clinton (A-Texas)	.059	6	17	4	1	1	0	0	2	0
Chris Curry	Conway	C	Norwich (AA-San Francisco)	.111	13	36	2	4	1	0	0	1	0
John Paul Davis	Russellville	1B	Visalia (A-Tampa Bay)	.218	25	78	14	17	2	0	2	9	4
Brent Blugach	UALR	SS	W. Michigan (A-Detroit)	.284	29	109	18	31	8	2	2	9	3
Matt Erickson	Arkansas	PH	Nashville (AAA-Milwaukee)	.429	10	7	1	3	0	0	0	2	0
Melvin Falu	Southern Arkansas	2B	Newark (Independent)	.429	8	28	5	12	1	1	0	1	0
Rick Guarno	UALR	C	Modesto (A-Colorado)	.400	2	5	2	2	0	0	0	0	2
Cedrick Harris	Ashdown	LF	Edinburg (Independent)	.286	5	21	2	6	0	0	0	0	2
Will Lewis	Texarkana	LF	W. Virginia (A-Milwaukee)	.330	27	91	10	30	5	1	3	23	3
Bryant Nelson	Crossett	2B	Syracuse (AAA-Toronto)	.313	32	128	16	40	4	1	1	13	1
Rodney Nye	Arkansas	3B	Norfolk (AAA-N.Y. Mets)	.316	15	38	8	12	3	1	1	8	1
Kit Pellow	Arkansas	DH	Tacoma (AAA-Seattle)	.417	4	12	3	5	1	0	1	3	0
Corey Ragsdale	Jonesboro	SS	St Lucis (A-N.Y. Mets)	.227	28	110	17	25	3	3	4	16	4
Matt Rogelstad	ASU	3B	Inland Empire (A-Mariners)	.372	29	121	17	45	7	0	0	17	2
S. Smitherman	UALR	3B	Louisville (AAA-Cincinnati)	.255	29	106	9	27	8	0	0	9	1
Terry Tiffee	NLR	3B	Rochester (AAA-Minnesota)	.267	15	60	11	16	2	1	3	9	0
Geraldo Valentin	Southern Arkansas	SS	Burlinton (A-Kansas City)	.320	27	103	17	33	5	2	1	12	2
Andrew Wishy	Arkansas	LF	Clinton (A-Texas)	.208	26	77	12	16	4	0	1	7	1

Major League Position Players

PLAYER	COLLEGE/HOMETOWN	POS	TEAM (CLASS-ORG)	AVG	G	AB	R	H	2B	3B	HR	RBI	SB
Eric Hinske	Arkansas	3B	Toronto	.281	33	114	26	32	8	1	4	20	3
Torii Hunter	Pine Bluff	OF	Minnesota	.248	32	121	19	30	7	0	4	18	11
Terry Tiffee	NLR	3B	Minnesota	.250	13	40	5	10	4	0	1	7	0

Minor League Pitchers

PLAYER	COLLEGE/HOMETOWN	POS	TEAM (CLASS-ORG)	W-L	ERA	G	GS	SV	IP	H	BB	SO
Clint Brannon	Bradford	P	Bakersfield (A-Texas)	2-2	5.40	7	1	0	20.0	22	7	15
Matt Carnes	Arkansas	P	Durham (AAA-Tampa Bay)	2-0	2.79	13	0	0	19.1	19	4	16
Brad Cherry	Texarkana	P	Chattanooga (AA-Cincinnati)	0-2	7.71	7	0	0	9.1	15	3	8
Paxton Crawford	Morrilton	P	Long Island (Independent)	3-0	1.35	3	3	0	20.0	14	1	7
Jarrett Gardner	Arkansas	P	Wilmington (A-Boston)	0-2	7.31	6	5	0	28.1	40	3	24
Steve Green	Arkansas-Monticello	P	Akron (AA-Cleveland)	0-2	4.74	11	0	1	19.0	17	13	22
Daniel Haigwood	Pleasant Plains	P	Winston Salem (A-Chi. White Sox)	4-1	3.38	7	7	0	32.0	35	14	35
Adam Haren	Maumelle	P	Fort Myers (A-Minnesota)	2-3	5.04	6	6	0	30.1	30	21	25
Thomas Hendricks	Jacksonville	P	Fort Worth (Independent)	0-0	2.84	2	0	0	6.1	3	1	5
Charlie Isaacson	Arkansas	P	Columbus (AAA-N.Y. Yankees)	0-0	6.75	7	0	0	10.2	19	7	7
Scott Roehl	Arkansas	P	Lake County (A-Cleveland)	1-2	3.00	11	0	0	18.0	18	6	16
John Sawatski	Little Rock	P	Fort Myers (A-Minnesota)	1-0	0.00	11	0	4	18.0	14	2	15

Major League Pitchers

PLAYER	COLLEGE/HOMETOWN	POS	TEAM (CLASS-ORG)	W-L	ERA	G	GS	SV	IP	H	BB	SO
A.J. Burnett	NLR	P	Florida	3-3	2.70	7	7	0	50.0	43	14	52
Cliff Lee	Benton	P	Cleveland	4-1	4.24	7	7	0	40.1	41	7	25
Matt Whiteside	ASU	P	Toronto	0-0	18.00	1	0	0	2.0	3	2	2

CHAPTER 5

*Every year the senior class picks a day to skip school and plan a social outing. The annual tradition is known as **senior skip day**. Even though the school staff alays seems to know when skip day is, the seniors don't seem to get in much trouble because it is only considered an unexcused absence. The seniors thought long and hard about the date then finally decided on March 18.*

Traditionally many of the seniors get together on this day to hang out or do something wild and crazy to flex their rebellious side. Seniors Mieisha Jackson and Braylon Harris met their friends at Check E cheese. Jackson said, "We were able to be kids again and not feel bad about it.

Nothing spectabcular happened, except that we got kicked out. Altogether the day was fun."

Although this day was supposed to be a relaxing and enjoyable day away from high school, many seniors used this day to work. Senior Dallas Sullivan did just that. He said, "I had to work my job at Kroger. If I hadn't worked I would have driven to Hot Springs and hung out downtown."

Many senior[s] were disappointed that they could not participate in the annual tradition. Senior TC Squires, a member of the varsity baseball team said, "I made sure that I was at school for at least half a day even though the games ended up being canceled."

Many seniors participated by enjoying the time away from the stresses of school. Good planning positioned the skip day right before spring break, giving seniors one more day off.[20]

My state of mind was somewhere between hope and despair. Despite starting all nine games up to this point, my batting average was in the low .200s. Although my on-base percentage was decent, I knew I had to work harder. Like most of my team, I had a slow start. I was making good contact and having good vision, but I was frustrated by some unlucky breaks, such as line drives caught, fair balls called foul, foul balls called fair, and long and tough battles fighting off pitches. Nevertheless, I tried to stay positive and focus on the solid hits I had, including that long double off the big blue wall at home. If

I had hit it with a little more power or a slightly higher launch angle, the ball would have been gone.

Conference play was approaching, and I was ready to give my best performance. However, Coach had different plans. Before we took on Jonesboro, Coach Foor called me to the front of the bus, where he and Coach Tipton were waiting. They asked what I thought about my progress, and I told them about my improvement in hitting and fielding. I was relieved to know that I was starting each game, unlike the previous year when I didn't know if I was going to be the designated hitter. But the conversation took an unexpected turn when Coach told me that he wanted to give Nathan a chance to prove himself at third. Although I had done fine, he thought it would only be fair to let Nathan have a chance since he had recovered from a back strain.

I was confused and disappointed. Did Coach really care about being fair? We were starting conference this week. Shouldn't we put the best lineup in the game? Nathan hadn't played all season, whereas I had put in five or more hours a day to be at my best. How could this be happening?

I wanted to express all of this, but I held back. I was in a state of shock, and I knew that my words wouldn't make any difference. It was always Coach's plan to replace me with Nathan. Nathan was the starting third baseman last year while I was the designated hitter for him. I made a mistake on the bases, and Nathan hit a home run the next inning. I never played again. This season was no different. Starting me during non-conference play was just for show. If I did well, Coach could take credit, and if I failed, he had a backup plan to cover his losses. I left the front of the bus defeated, and my confidence hit an all-time low. All those long hours spent working on my swing and running were not enough.

Thursday, March 20, 2008
Jonesboro Golden Hurricanes @ Sylvan Hills
Conference Doubleheader

The atmosphere crackled with excitement. Banners and flags fluttered in the sunshine as the pressbox blared *"Centerfield"* by John Fogerty during our pre-game warmup. Coach's dad, Mr. Jerry Tipton, grilled burgers with his wife at our makeshift concession area, always wearing a smile and supporting us every chance he got. There was nowhere better to be on a Thursday afternoon.

It was finally time for the battle-tested, yet underperforming, Sylvan Hills Bears to face off against conference rivals Jonesboro. Despite the two-hour trip from Hurricane Drive, Jonesboro's confidence was likely at its peak after their tumultuous start. Just a year prior, in Jonesboro, *"the Bears salvaged a split with the Hurricane with a 6-1 win in the nightcap after blowing a 3-0 lead late in game one . . . Shod Neely scored the final run of the game in the fifth inning off a sac fly by T.C.*

Squires . . . .After Searcy and Sylvan Hills, Jonesboro is in third place at 7 - 3."[21] While Sylvan Hills eventually finished as Conference Champs, Jonesboro's comeback haunted us for the rest of that season as we barely edged out a Bye in the tournament.

This year, we weren't playing for a split. We wanted it all. Although I knew I wouldn't start, I still hoped for a chance to pinch-hit, take over at third if Nathan was called on to pitch in relief, or even DH the second game should someone have a bad night. But that opportunity never came.

They (Sylvan Hills) started off with four runs in the bottom of the first inning, and added another in the third before putting it out of reach in the fifth inning with five more.

D.J. Baxendale dominated for Sylvan Hills. The former Abundant Life standout hurler gave up only one hit through five innings while striking out eight batters. Offensively, he went 3-of-3 with five RBI, including a two-run home run in the bottom of the fifth following singles by Clint Thornton and Mark Turpin. Nathan Eller had two hits in the opener, while Thornton added two in the nightcap.

"D.J. pitched a really good game for us," Tipton said. "He's had some struggles, to be honest, but he really come through for us (Thursday.) Chambers has been playing quite a bit of outfield for us, and has helped us out a lot." The third former Owl, Justin Treece, has not seen action yet this year due to a broken hand.[22]

Game 1 was an absolute slaughter; what a showing! A five-inning run-rule in the first conference game of the season. We couldn't have asked for a better start, but we couldn't celebrate yet. Just like in 2007, Jonesboro was out for revenge and wanted to split the series again. As we learned last year, every conference game counts. Only a few wins could separate the top-ranked teams to get the Byes, and arms to pitch were always at a premium come tournament time. Hunter started the second game of the series.

The Bears took the early lead with a run in the top of the first inning, but the Hurricane came back with a pair of runs in the bottom half. Sylvan Hills answered with two runs in the third and another in the fourth that gave them a 4-2 lead.

The Hurricane entered the seventh inning of game two trailing 5-3, and quickly put their first batters on with singles. A passed ball made it 5-4, but Ole Miss signee Hunter Miller made the play of the game to preserve the win when he threw out the potential game-tying run trying to score from second on a base hit.

The game ended on a grounder to short as the Bears improved to 8-4 overall and 2-0 in the conference. Sylvan Hills reliever Jake Chambers took to the mound for the Bears in the seventh inning. Hunter Miller started and got the win before giving way to Chris Daulton in the fifth inning.

"The second game was a completely

different ballgame altogether," Sylvan Hills coach Denny Tipton said. "It was a game of blown opportunities. It's good anytime you can get two wins in conference, but it was touch and go there for a while."

Sylvan Hills started its 6A-East Conference campaign strong on Thursday at Kevin McReynolds Field, sweeping league rival Jonesboro, 10-0 and 5-4

"We need to swing the bat better overall as a team," Tipton said. "That's the main thing holding us back right now. Clint Thornton is the one that's really swinging the bat for us right now. The last three games, he has hit really well."[22]

The Bears have not swept conference rival Jonesboro in years but, thanks to great teamwork and effort, the team won these two games 10, 5 to 0, 4. D.J. Baxenale was perhaps the biggest help to the team pitching a shut-out in game one and going 5 for 8 with a home run.

Hunter Miller started the second game pitching 4 innings and gave up 4 runs. Chris Daulton was in relief of Miller and pitched until Jake Chambers came in the game to close it in the 7th inning. Miller saved the game when he threw out the tying run from center field.[23]

And just like that, we were 2-0 in conference play with a strong showing of power in the first game and a tough display of depth in the second. Jonesboro would have to sulk and wait another year for a chance at redemption. In the meantime, we were already looking towards our next conference challenger, Mountain Home.

Tuesday, March 25th
Sylvan Hills @ Mountain Home Bombers
Conference Doubleheader

The week of Spring Break did n't mean a break from baseball. Even without school, we continued to work out and practice, fully focused on the game we loved. The three-hour bus ride to Mountain Home didn't faze us, and we went into the game relaxed.

The second conference game was against [Mountain Home] who already lost to Jonesboro the week before. The bears knew this game could be too easy but they still planned to play their hardest and did just that. The bears won the first game 25 to 3. Ace pitcher D.J. Baxendale pitched the first inning, but then was pulled to be saved for game two. Relief pitcher Jake Chambers came in to pitch until Chris Perez closed this one in the 5th inning."[24]

It was an absolute hit barrage that ended the game early. A few days off of school and some laid back fun at practice did wonders for us on the ball field.

"Game two wasn't a blowout like the game

before, but it too ended early due to the run rule
after 5 innings of play. The Bears won this one
10-0 in six innings with Baxendale pitching four
innings and Miller the last two." [24]

Sylvan Hills moved to 11 - 4 overall and 4 - 0 in conference play. We stayed tied in the 6A East with Marion.

Friday, March 29th

Game 1: Sylvan Hills vs. Conway Wampus Cats

Saturday, March 30th

Game 2: Sylvan Hills vs. Fort Smith Southside Rebels
Game 3: Sylvan Hills vs. Conway Wampus Cats
Conway Invitational Tournament

A weekend tournament in Conway wrapped up our Spring Break. We faced off against the hosting Wampus Cats in our first game of the set, followed by a game against Fort Smith Southside. Winning those two games would set us up for the third game, which coincidentally brought us back to Conway. All our games were against 7A powerhouse teams. With the quick turnaround from the tournament for our next conference games against West Memphis, Coach would have to be careful with our starters' pitch counts.

Hunter Miller, the Ole Miss football signee, was all that on Friday afternoon in Sylvan Hills' 12-5 win over Conway in a round-robin tournament at Conway High School. Sylvan Hills jumped out to a 16-6 lead against Southside on Saturday, then held off a late rally. The Bears pounded out 17 more hits, including three by Baxendale and Thorton. Miller added two hits and four RBI, including a home run. Chambers, Perez, Spears and Turpin also chipped in two hits apiece.[25]

After sitting out games against Jonesboro, Mountain Home, Conway, and Fort Smith Southside, I finally got another start. In the final game of the tournament, Nathan was called on to pitch as we had used Spears, Miller, D.J., and Chambers in the first two wins of the weekend. One game required the team to battle back before taking a convincing lead in the seventh, followed by another where we jumped out to an early lead before letting them close the gap. Both games were littered with hits and bang-bang plays.

I wish I could say I made a great showing against Conway. I wish I could say I earned that starting spot back during that game. That's not what happened. Early in the game, Conway hit a routine fly ball to me at third base. It was a guaranteed out. I had taken countless fly balls almost exactly like this. It should have been an easy, but instead, the ball landed in the palm of my glove and fell to the ground, much to the team and crowd's dismay. I picked it up quickly, but there wasn't a play at first.

Immediately, thoughts of failure rushed in. I had high hopes for myself for this game. I wanted to show that I was still worthy of playing the game of baseball, and I missed the easiest play for me. I'm surprised Coach didn't pull me right then, but there wasn't another third baseman on the team. Lock was technically the next man up, but my defensive skills, arm, and bat were lightyears ahead of him at the time. I'm sure McKinney or Ryan would have jumped at the chance, but neither had ever played third base and were in a similar situation as Lock. They wouldn't have known the plays from that position versus second base. So, I stayed in the game.

Unlike the slower start of the first Conway game, we were on fire during this one. We were close to run-ruling them by the time I stepped up to bat for the second time. It had been about two weeks since I faced game-speed pitching, so every swing was late on the ball. I fouled off multiple pitches, but couldn't get around on anything inside. With runners on base and two outs, I was able to flare one into right field just in front of the fielder for a single. A hit! It felt great. It wasn't the best swing, but late in the count, it showed Coach that I was still capable of getting a clutch hit.

The next batter walked up and took the signs from Coach. We had a substantial lead at this point, so I was watching but not expecting anything. Even though I had worked on my speed all off-season, I still wasn't a base-stealing expert. I thought it was a swing-away situation. Tipton went through the signs as usual, moving his left and right hands up and down from his legs and chest to shoulders and head, ending with a clap. Among the almost random motions, Coach had hidden the steal sign. Not just any steal sign, but a delayed steal. It was one of the four steals we practiced all season: straight steal, leave early, three-quarter, and delay.

To perform a delayed steal, the pitcher would come set, and on his movement to the plate, the runner on first would take two large secondary hops while the ball traveled home. As soon as the runner came down from that second hop, it was a mad rush to second base. The whole point was to catch the defense off-guard and out of position or disrupt the first-and-third play call from the other team.

I looked over at Coach Foor while standing on first base. He walked over and whispered, *"Did you get the sign?"* I nodded, *"Yes, I got it."* I understood what I was supposed to do, but I didn't understand why I was stealing. We had a good lead, and the team was hitting the ball really well. The call didn't make sense to me, but Coach Tipton had his reasons for giving the sign.

The catcher came out and made similar signals to what Tipton made at third and turned back to take his place behind home plate. I began my lead—three full steps off of first, a crouch, and two more small shuffles away from the bag. Our runner on third took his lead. I wasn't too concerned about a pickoff, but I was close enough to get back on a quick move or a fake third-to-first throw. Neither happened. The pitcher came set, lifted his leg to go home, and I started my secondary lead—one big shuffle, second big shuffle. The ball was heading toward home. My foot hit the ground, and I took off to second. In the 3.5 seconds it took to get from my leadoff position to second base, I watched the fielder catch the ball right in front of my foot as I slid in for the third out of the inning.

Coach yelled from third base as I looked over to see him the most angry I had ever seen. His face was burning red, and he was coming across the field screaming at me about how I had cost us another run. I wasn't sure what to do or say. Did I do something wrong? It was the right sign—delay steal. I didn't even hear his words anymore as I tried to figure out what I had missed. I picked myself up and ran back to the dugout to grab my glove and get back on the field. Before I could leave the dugout, Coach yelled for someone else to take my place at third base. I was embarrassed. I couldn't understand what I did wrong.

It wasn't until later in the game that one of the other players told me that I should have peeked to see if the catcher was throwing down to second. Then I could have gotten into a rundown so the runner could score from third. I don't remember that being part of our delay steal practice—for the three-quarter steal, yes. Maybe I missed it, or that was something the faster players had worked on without me. The whole play didn't make sense. It felt like I was set up to fail. If Coach wanted me in a rundown, then we have a three-quarter steal exactly for that situation, or we could have let the batter hit. We didn't need the run. The final score was a blowout. It was at this point that I started to feel like it wasn't just me failing the team. I felt like I had been failed.

I threw my glove in my bag and took off my cleats. I hid in the top corner of the dugout so the fans couldn't see me and to stay out of the way of the rest of the team. I remember my dad coming over to look for me. He was angry that Coach Tipton had yelled at me in front of the other players and their families. Dad asked if I wanted him to take me home right then, and I said no. Instead, I sulked in the dugout, only leaving it at the end of the game to shake hands.

> *Eller took the win in the second contest with Conway. Turpin went 4 for 4, while Baxendale was 3 for 3. Miller picked up another home run and two more hits, and Long added two base knocks, as well.*
>
> *"Our bats started off really slow this seasons," said Bears head coach Denny Tipton. "But the last seven games, we're really swinging it well."*
>
> *As in 92 runs over that span, while limiting opponents to just 28. Sylvan Hills, which walloped Mountain Home 25-3 and 10-0 last Tuesday, is now 13-4 overall. All four of those losses are by single runs.*[24]
>
> *The Bears won the Conway tournament over Spring Break. The Bears averaged 13.6 runs per game, beating Conway in games one and three and Fort Smith Southside in game two.*
>
> *The coaches attribute the bears offesne with the wins. "The bats really have been coming to life lately," said Coach Tipton. "I hope we can keep it up."*
>
> *The Bears seem to be "unbeatable" when they play together. Defense and pitching has been*

the key to the Bears success, but when they add great hitting, the possibilities are endless.[23]

Saturday, May 5th, 2007
West Memphis Blue Devils vs. Sylvan Hills
Semifinals of the State Tournament
@ Harding University

Texarakana, Benton, Lake Hamilton and Watson Chapel from the South, and Sylvan Hills and Jonesboro from the East all have to be considered contenders for the crown this year.[25]

There's something to be said about a revenge game in baseball. This series had been circled on the calendar for almost a year. West Memphis was the team we were after. The taste of a bad loss in the 2007 State Tournament against a team that we had beaten twice earlier in conference play still lingered. To a lot of people, we were a laughing stock after our poor showing. Radio announcers talked about it for weeks after the beatdown, almost more so than the actual State Championship Game.

The Junior Class
of
Sylvan Hills High School

Requests the honor of your presence
at the

"Diamonds Are Forever"
Junior & Senior Prom 2007

on Friday, May 4, 2007
at seven-thirty p.m.

Grand March at six p.m.

Woman's City Club
401 South Scott Street
Little Rock, Arkansas

Diamonds Are Forever
S.H.H.S. Prom 2007

Our last game against the Blue Devils was in the State semi-final round of the tournament. We clinched a first-round Bye during our last conference games, allowing us to avoid a Friday game. This was a big deal because Friday night was Sylvan Hills' Junior & Senior Prom. For months, we had planned the event—getting dates, renting tuxes and limos, and preparing for a great night. Somehow, it was overlooked that the 1st round of the tournament started on that Friday. Coach told us weeks before that if we didn't get the Bye, we would have to miss Prom. Heartbreak. Not just for us, but for our dates, the money spent, and the lost time. My date went to a different high school and had offers to go to her Prom on the same night, but she was going with me instead. I know others had similar issues. I can't say going to Prom was the only driver for us to win the Conference, but it didn't hurt. Sure enough, that's what we did, and on that Friday, we had a grand night in downtown Little Rock.

Our problem came the following day when we had to ride the bus to Harding University to face off against conference foe West Memphis. Getting on the bus, we could tell there was something off about the team. We weren't the usual rowdy bunch. The noon gametime and the Prom "hangover" were going to be a problem, and it didn't take long for it to show.

They went down 2-0 in the top of the first inning, as the Bears gave up two runs right off the bat. Things went just as poorly for Sylvan Hills at the plate early in the game. Three-hole hitter Hunter Miller had a pitch behind his back hit the bat and roll fair, where it was scooped up and thrown to first almost before Miller realized the ball was in play. Amazingly, it was only the first of two wild pitches in the game that careened of Bear bats.

Leading 4-1, West Memphis added three more runs on a three-RBI dinger by Jackson Smith. The three were runs were unearned, as a two-out error at short kept the inning alive. Stewart Warner reached with a two-out single to start the fourth-inning rally before Scarborough reahed on the E6.

"We got off to a bad start and just never could catch a break," Sylvan Hills coach Denny Tipton said. "I still wasn't really worried though until the Jackson kid hit that home run that put them up 7-1. I started thinking we might be in trouble then."

The lead grew to 10-1 in the top of the sixth, but the Bears got out of what was almost a mercy rule ending. Jackson Smith, TJ Holt and Hardage walked the bases loaded with no outs. Harrell then hit a fly to shallow right field that wasn't deep enough to score Smith from third, but Quentin Smith singled to right to drive in two runs.

The Bears threatened to rally in the bottom of the sixth, but managed just one run despite putting runners on second and third with one out and running Hardage off the mound.

Tony Pavan led off with a triple down the

right field line and scored on a single by Thornton. Nathan Eller and Roark then walked and moved up a base each on a wild pitch. That drove starting pitcher McCully Hardage off the mound and to third base, where he would prove just as instrumental.

Turpin then struck out, and bad luck again reared its ugly head for the Bears. Miller pulled a hard line drive down the third base line that was snagged by Hardage, who turned and stepped on the bag to double up Eller and end the inning.

Roark took the mound in the seventh and sat the Devils down in order, but the Bears couldn't score in the bottom half of the frame, despite putting the first two batters on base.

Sylvan Hills left 13 runners on base and had two runners caught on the base paths in the game. West Memphis doubled Sylvan Hills hit total with 12 base raps, and committed no errors compared the Sylvan Hills' three miscues.

"I thought my kids never quit, they just couldn't get a break" Tipton said. "I thought we had a great year. We won conference with a lot of new faces and a lot of people picking us not to win it this year. I told them to not judge their season on one game. We had a great year, we're conference champs and we did a lot of things that we can build off of next season." [26]

The Dynasty Continues

2007 - Conference Champs, ... TBA
2006 - Conference Champs, State Quarterfinals
2005 - STATE CHAMPS
2004 - Conference Champs, State Runner-up
2003 - Conference Champs, STATE CHAMPS
2002 - Conference Champs, State Semifinals
2001 - Conference Champs, State Semifinals
2000 - Conference Champs, State Semifinals
OVERALL RECORDS
CONFERENCE 95-18   PLAYOFFS 20-5

We were a disaster. Despite being the 6A East Conference Champions, our title didn't translate to the game. We committed three errors, left thirteen players on bases, had pitchers who couldn't throw strikes, and suffered from a bunch of bad breaks. We didn't deserve to win. West Memphis did. They played their best baseball at the right time and beat Benton before beating us. West Memphis advanced to the 6A Championship game at Baum, where they ultimately lost 3-4 to Texarkana. This is why the series against West Memphis was so important. It had been a year in the making, and we needed to prove that semi-final game in the State Tournament was a fluke.

Tuesday, April 1st, 2008
West Memphis Blue Devils @ Sylvan Hills
Conference Doubleheader

Another conference doubleheader, another double romp. The Sylvan Hills Bears remained perfect in 6A Conference play on Wednesday afternoon by walloping last year's state runner-up West Memphis, 12-0 and 16-2, at Sherwood Parks. The victories — the Bears' ninth and tenth consecutive — improved them to 15-4 overall, 6-0 in conference play and tied with Marion for first place. The Patriots took two from Jacksonville on Wednesday to move to 6-0. Over the past nine games, Sylvan Hills has outscored its opponents 120-30. Bears head coach Denny Tipton said he's not too worried about his team going unchallenged over the past several weeks.

"We've had some close games," he said, noting the Bears escaped with a 5-4 win over Jonesboro in a sweep of the Hurricane to open league play. "But these are a lot easier on the coach."

Sylvan Hills four losses this season have been by one run each — two in extra innings. Extra innings were not an issue on Wednesday. In fact, both games ended early. D.J. Baxendale was untouchable in the opener, losing a no-hitter in the fifth when Michael Harrell led off the fifth and final inning with a looper that dropped in for West Memphis' only hit.

"D.J. has pitched well for us all year," Tipton said of the junior transfer from Abundant Life who has already committed to Missouri State. "That's his third one-hitter in conference and in all of them, they seem to get a little Texas Leaguer on him. I think in all his conference games, they've only hit two balls out of the infield on him."

With a fastball nearing 90 miles per hour, and a wicked slider and curve ball to go along with it, Baxendale (6-1) had the Blue Devils waving awkwardly all night. Baxendale struck out nine and walked only one.[27]

In Game 1, we capitalized on our opportunities in the first, utilizing four walks, two wild pitches, and Jake's two-run single to build a 4-0 lead. We extended our lead to a quick 10-0 in the second inning, courtesy of another RBI single from Jake and a two-run double from Blake, who continued to contribute with an RBI double to the center field fence in the fourth inning. Clint Thornton brought him home with a single.

We only managed seven hits in the first game, but our bats came alive in the second, producing 14 more. In the first, Hunter delivered an RBI single and Baxendale brought in another run with a sacrifice fly, giving Sylvan Hills a 2-0 lead. We added three more runs in the second inning, highlighted by Spears' sacrifice fly and RBI singles from Miller and Baxendale, extending our lead to 5-0.

"We've been hitting pretty good one through nine," Tipton said. "That's the key and that's what I tell them: Don't panic. If it's not your night to hit, somebody else will pick it up. We're pretty consistent up and down the lineup. When we all hit on the same night, we're pretty good."[27]

After going down in order in the third inning, Sylvan

Hills exploded in the fourth, sending 11 batters to the plate and scoring six runs. The highlight of the inning was Miller's two-run homer to left-center. Miller finished the game 3 for 4 with four RBIs. Jake contributed a two-run single, and Evans added an RBI single in the fourth.

D.J. and Hunter combined for a 6-for-7 performance with seven RBIs in the second game. Even the bottom of our order was contributing. Jake, Blake, and Spears, who occupied the seventh, eighth, and ninth spots in the lineup, each had two hits. Jake drove in three runs. West Memphis managed to avoid a five-inning run rule by scoring two runs with two outs in the fifth inning, narrowing the deficit to 11-2 and prolonging the game.

However, we didn't let up and continued our offensive onslaught in the top of the sixth, sending ten more batters to the plate and scoring five runs. Turpin delivered a two-run double, while Jake contributed an RBI double, and Baxendale added an RBI single.

On the mound, Hunter allowed four hits, three walks, and two earned runs over five innings, striking out four batters. He brought his record up to 3-1. Chambers closed out the game in impressive fashion, striking out all three West Memphis batters he faced in the sixth inning.

Sylvan Hills defeated West Memphis 12-0 and 16-2 on Wednesday. Ten games ago, the Bears were just 5-4. Sylvan Hills coach Denny Tipton was also wondering at the time when his offense was going to wake up and come around. he wins kept the Bears perfect in league play at 6-0 and moved the team to 15-4 overall. Well, the Bears have now outscored their opponents 120-30 over the past nine games. Fort Smith Southside scored 13 of those runs in a game where the Bears had built a sizable lead and were pitching the 10th and 11th.

The Sylvan Hills Bears won what turned out to be the final home games of the season in impressive fashion. The Bears still had home games left on the schedule, but all have become road games . . .[28]

CHAPTER 6

After Spring Break, we spent a few days re-adjusting to classroom life. Then on Thursday night, the sirens started blaring. Unaware of the weather, my dad called and urged me to get home as quickly as possible because there were thunderstorms or worse on the way. Our house, which was raised off the ground, was the safest place to ride out the storm. When I got home, my family were glued to the news which was reporting a tornado warning. We were upgraded to a tornado watch shortly after. We gathered some essentials—flashlights, blankets, and snacks—and hurriedly rushed beneath the house. The wind picked up, and the news reports grew worse, informing us that a tornado had touched down in Sherwood. It was near the edge of Camp Robinson then the North Little Rock Municipal Airport, heading east. We lived close to the middle of town, not in the immediate area, but we were advised to take cover. When the sirens finally ended, we went back upstairs, unsure of what to expect the next morning.

Hundreds of central Arkansas residents emerged from shelters and their homes Friday, many amazed by the damage that at least two tornadoes left behind the night before. By midmorning residents were outside, busily sawing and moving trees that had fallen on houses or cars and assessing the wreckage that spread for miles from Saline to Pulaski count[y].

Gov. Mike Beebe toured storm-damaged parts of central Arkansas later in the day, offering comfort to residents and bemoaning the latest in a series of weather shocks to hit the state in the past two months.

A storm system Thursday night - caused by the collision of a cold front with areas of intense moisture - spawned the tornadoes and resulted in miles of damage from Bryant to Little Rock, its suburbs and beyond. One of the twisters destroyed mobile homes in Benton, and another tossed around planes at North Little Rock Municipal Airport. Heavy rain caused more flooding throughout the region.

On Friday, Beebe declared five counties disaster areas - Arkansas, Garland, Saline, Pulaski and St. Francis. The action - increasing the number of counties declared disaster areas to

44 - will be included in the governor's previous request for federal disaster assistance related to recent flooding.

"It's heart-wrenching to see the tornadic activity and the damage and the flooding and then we get more tornadoes and more flooding - the damage not just to the physical property, not just the loss of lives and not just the injuries that occur but what it does to the morale, what it does to the emotions of the families, those that have lost their own possessions that are irreplaceable," the governor said. "You know, some things can be replaced, but then there are memories and there are things handed down by your parents and grandparents that just can't be replaced."

The cold front that caused the storms was expected to move out of the state overnight, leaving dry conditions and allowing residents a brief respite from the rain as they begin the cleanup process, said Emilie Nipper, forecaster with the weather service. Another front should be moving into the area next week, causing more rain to fall Tuesday through Thursday, Nipper said.

Thursday's tornadoes were the latest in a series of blows struck by Mother Nature this year. A tornado in January killed one man. Feb. 5 brought two more tornadoes, killing 13 people. One tore a 123-mile swath from Yell County to Sharp County. Early March brought as much as a foot of snow in some places in Arkansas, while mid-March flooding caused rivers to spill out of their banks and inundate entire towns. Two died in the flooding, and one man remains missing.

At the peak of the storm Friday morning, Entergy Arkansas Inc. had about 45,000 customers without power, but by afternoon that number had been reduced to 8,000, an Entergy spokesman said. The hardest-hit areas were Little Rock, Hot Springs, Cabot, Jacksonville and Conway. The Little Rock Zoo closed Friday because of a power failure. More than 300 workers were on the ground by the afternoon repairing more than 60 broken utility poles, 100 crossbeams and 125

spans of wire across the state, he said. Though crews made steady progress, Thompson estimated that most of the power won't be restored until tonight - and possibly not before Sunday for some rural areas.[29]

Friday, we woke up to the news that school would be cancelled due to storm damage. Multiple tornadoes had ripped through Sylvan Hills Optimist, crossed the high school, and blown through the neighborhoods north of the school. I wanted to drive up to see the damage, but the police had blocked off the streets as it wasn't safe for regular travel. Trees were down everywhere, and there was no power in the area.

Sylvan Hills was shocked on April 3rd when a series of devastating storms including a F2 tornado with winds between 111-135 mph swept through Central Arkansas including parts of Sherwood. One of the places hardest hit was Sylvan Hills High School, which sustained damages of an estimated $750,000 to the auditorium, the football field, and several classrooms.

Roof damage to the main building caused major flooding on the second floor and the family and consumer science classes just below. Classrooms occupied by Mr. Burns, Mrs. Evans, Mrs. Tripp, Mrs. Rice, Mrs. A. Harris, and Mrs. Atkinson, as well as Mrs. Lipsmeyer's office, all sustained major losses because of water damage. Computers, desks, textbooks, bookshelves, and years of lecture notes are among the items being dried out before educators and students can attmept to reuse them.

Roof damage also caused the 300-Building to be declared off-limits to student occupation. Damage to that building will require a new roof, new ceiling tiles, and insulation. According to Mr. Rushing, thirty-three computers were damaged in the 300-Building along with numerous textbooks, testing booklets, and other teaching materials. Repairs on this building are near the top of the priority list because of displaced students; May 1 has been mentioned as the latest possible date of completion.

The Choir room was also flooded - the sound system, countless sheets of music, and a piano were destroyed by the storm. Days of rain following the tornado had Mrs. Elaine Harris wading into her room trying to salvage teaching materials for the rest of the year.

The tornado's winds were so vicious that they peeled the roof completely off the south side of the auditorium. This allowed the rain to pour in, soaking all of the stagecraft equipment and the wood that was going to be used to build the set for the spring play. Mr. Dupins said "We are going to have the spring play no matter what! If we can not perform at the Jim Burgett auditorium then the play will be performed at the North Pulaski auditorium with bus transportation as if it were a field trip."

They gym was also significantly damaged. The roof was lifted off the building then set back down a few inches cockeyed. This left a 4-6 inch gap allowing flooding in the locked rooms and debris to cover the gym floor. Engineers must check the integrity of the building to make sure it wasn't compromised before students will be allowed back inside.

Bill Blackwood stadium did not escape unscathed. It too sustained moderate damage. Several of the light poles were blown down. This created a danger because live electrical lines were lying within anyone's reach. Coach Johnny Rice said, "It wasn't all bad because we needed new ones anyway." Because repairs at the football field are lower on the priority list than of educational needs, the soccer teams will not be playing on the field for the rest of their season.

The torando caused extensive damage to the school and caused many people's lives to be disrupted, but it could have been much worse. Positive attitudes are helping things move along.[30]

Nearly 1,000 Sylvan Hills High School students will be displaced next week because of significant storm damage to the building in Sherwood.

Classes were canceled Friday and will remain so until Thursday, when the students will be shuffled to other facilities in the area to resume their lessons. Sylvan Hills middle and elementary schools - as well as Northwood and Cato elementaries were closed Friday because they had no electricity, but they may reopen Monday if power is restored.[31]

I wasn't worried about returning to class as much as returning to baseball. My GPA and grades were all but sealed in this final semester. Getting on the field again, that's what was on my mind the most, and that's when Coach called.

The day after the tornado, Sylvan Hills Head Baseball Coach Denny Tipton called all the

players together at his home. He informed them what had happened with damage to the field and the loss of equipment. At that point, the team's motto became, No Excuses. This phrase was used over and over in the coming months. The baseball team had T-shirts made with the motto. The players would tell each other, No Excuses often.[32]

Sylvan Hills High School (Sherwood, Ark) was hit with an F-3 tornado April 3—which packed 158-206 mph winds and caused millions of dollars worth of destruction in the community, including the school's baseball facility.[33]

Practice was cancelled until the danger could be assessed. During our team meeting. Coach shared with us some devastating news: J.T.'s house had been directly hit by the tornado. Fortunately, the family was safe and unharmed, but the house was destroyed. We planned to meet over the weekend in his neighborhood to salvage whatever we could and help them move into a new house down the road.

It caused damage to hundreds of houses. One of those houses hit was backup catcher J.T. Long. J.T. and his family had to stay with relatives because of the damage to their home. The Sylvan Hills baseball team came together and helped the Longs move all their valuables out of the damaged home.[32]

When we arrived, the sight was terrifying. The house was unrecognizable, with parts of the roof gone, water leaking through, and windows blown out. J.T. showed us the inner closet where he and his younger brother hid while the tornado passed over the house. There was a long plank sticking straight down through the ceiling, and we could see the sun through the hole. We packed boxes and picked up family keepsakes to carry down to the other house. The neighborhood was in the same shape —the damage substantial. Every home had something missing, broken, or sticking out from it. The area looked and felt strange, and then it hit us all at once: the trees were gone. We could see the sky in places where it was never visible before. Coach brought us information on the school. It was likely that we wouldn't be going back for a week or two. The administration was working on a plan, and our senior year was turning into a nightmare.

School remained closed on Monday as the cleanup continued. Officials worked on a plan to reopen the campus for at least some students. We were allowed to visit the baseball fields, but we had to park outside the main yellow gate and walk to the indoor facility and the rest of the park. The sight was haunting. Lines of downed trees split either side of the building. We could see the exact path of the tornados. A path of debris stretched across the parking lot toward the fields. Some of the field lights were no longer standing, creating a strange view of open sky. The five fields were arranged in a circle around a two-story concession stand and office building, but the second story was gone, except for a few remaining studs. We had no idea where they landed. All of the fences were blended with metal bleachers and pink insulation.

The main field where the high school and Legion games took place, was now unplayable . . . The 10 foot tall wood fences anchored in concrete were ripped out of the ground and thrown all around. Big chunks of turf were ripped out with structural damage to L-Screens, dugouts, and everything you could imagine.

"The morning after the tornado, high school baseball, football and Legion coaches searched in a cold rain for as much equipment as possible. Almost all of the equipment was either destroyed or lost all together. Damage to the Sports Complex was estimated at $1 million. We only found three bats. All of our helmets were dented and damaged and almost everything else had to be replaced. We had to purchase new bats, dozens of balls and new helmets. Some of *the damaged helmets we found were remarkable to look at. With the high winds of the tornado, several helmets smashed into trees, and they were folded inside out. Some of the helmets were found in the woods way past the sports complex. We figure close to $20,000 worth of equipment had to be replaced which included new catcher's gear, a medicine kit, amplifiers for the stadium and things like this." Foor said that the tornado also hit Sylvan Hills High School.[32]*

The baseball fields in Sherwood have been a place where visitors stare in awe at the talent displayed for years now.

Visitors to the park are staring in awe for a different reason now.

A tornado hit Sherwood hard on Thursday of last week and left the baseball fields in ruins. The fields have seen state champions from virtually every level of league play from t-ball up through high school and on to American Legion. The high school field was hit the hardest and has forced the Bears to move their remaining home games to the visitors' ballparks. The destruction is evident from any angle on the field.

Standing on the pitcher's mound on a normal day would have you looking at the press box directly in front of you, well behind home plate with a large amount of foul territory. Glancing to the right and you would see the home crowd cheering on another win while hamburgers

*and hot dogs are being grilled near the equipment
shed directly underneath the press box.*

*Glancing to the left and you would find
the visitors' stands with the concession stand and
main office in the background. Turning around
and facing the outfield nets a view of the big blue
wooden wall that stretches from foul pole to foul
pole.*[34]

Rounding field five towards the high school field, it was unrecognizable. The big blue wall with its Sherwood archers was all but gone, with only some of right field remaining. Roark's memorial banner in left field had also vanished. We could see all the way to the softball fields. The scorebox had barreled over the fence about thirty feet onto home plate, and the storage space beneath it had its contents scattered around. However, the donared 2-liters in storage underneath the box hadn't budged. The odds! The chain-link fence and bleachers were melded together, and the outdoor hitting cage down the left field line was gone. We couldn't believe what we were seeing. This was our home. Now there was nothing left. The power of nature had taken its toll on the team as we collected waterlogged baseballs and inspected the wooden practice mounds. Coach told us that they found the missing scoreboard in someone's backyard about a mile or so away.

The concession stand had a straight-line view of the high school auditorium, and the roof was missing over the right half. Letters were also missing from the Sylvan Hills High School sign across the front entrance. There were no words to describe the devastation.

Several sections of the Sylvan Hills High School roof were ripped off during Thursday's storm, allowing rainwater to pour in and flood the building, said James "Butch" Warren, the district's executive director of support services.

The roof of the auditorium is gone, and it appears that part of the auditorium's walls were lifted off the foundation, Warren said. The southwest corner of the building has major damage, and a computer lab was soaked.

Roof-top air-conditioning units were tossed to the ground. The entire campus is littered with tree branches, broken power poles and building debris, Warren said. Light poles near the football field were broken in half and flung across the bleachers. A city-owned baseball complex next to the school was destroyed.

The high school will be out of service for at least a few weeks, assuming the weather improves. Sections, including the auditorium, will be closed for the remainder of the year. Warren estimated that repairs to the building will cost several hundred thousand dollars.

School district administrators were scrambling Friday to find suitable classroom space for 920 high school students before classes resume Thursday.[31]

Electrical trucks surrounded the school, so we turned back toward the indoor facility and waited to hear our fate. The plan was fluid. Standardized testing was starting for the rest of the state while we were without a place to go. All we knew for certain was that we had to be back in class by Thursday. At first, we were told that enough classrooms were salvageable for the seniors to return to campus, while the sophomores and juniors were going to Woody's Sherwood Forest, and the freshmen to the Bill Harmon Recreational Center. Then, the seniors were going to be moved to the North Little Rock First Assembly of God, and the freshmen were going back to campus. However, a Tuesday meeting changed the plan again. This time it was set in stone: enough of the school, along with some trailers, had been opened so that all of the underclassmen could attend class at the high school, and seniors would continue at the Bill Harmon.

> *The winds that tore through central Arkansas Thursday night, terrorizing thousands huddled in their closets and bathrooms and snapping trees and power poles, also peeled back the roof at Sylvan Hills High School, sending Pulaski County Special School District officials scrambling to find alternative learning space for 920 students for the rest of the yar, according to James Warren, executive director for support services . . . "We're going to have to figure out transportation, food, how to get the stuff in school to the locations for the teachers . . . It's a huge operation," Warren said. "We've done it before and we can do it again. It looked like the hand of God reached down and pulled off the roof," Warren said of Sylvan Hills High*

School auditorium, and also of the roof over the computer lab, marinating computers in the rain and ruining them. The home economics lab was flooded and four classrooms were damaged. The math building was damaged and light poles broken in half at the football stadium. Metal roofing was wrapped around trees and poles, according to Warren. "This was the cleanest campus in the whole district," he added. "It now has a million pieces of paper scattered about." Warren, who learned of the Sylvan Hills catastrophe about 9:30 p.m. Thursday, was among those who worked through the night to address the problems.

A school bus driver who lived near the schools checked the damage and notified district officials. Those working to keep the high school going included Superintendent James Sharp, Beverly Ruthven, head of learning services, and district administrators Deborah Cooley, Rhonda Harnish and Bill Barnes and officials from Sherwood including Mayor Virginia Hillman, aldermen including Shelia Sulcer and Charlie Harmon, school board members Charlie Wood and Danny Gilliland and many others, Warren said. Former school board member Ronnie Calva, director of the Harmon Recreation Center, was there and offered use of the recreation center, according to Warren.

"I've never seen anything like the way the

city acted," said Warren. "Everybody who worked for Sherwood lined up and wanted to know 'what can we do to help?'" District security arrived to keep people out of the building and away from harm. On Friday, a team had to get food out of the school freezers and into frozen storage while it was still safe, he said. The new Sylvan Hills band room is also leaking, Warren said. "We'll be working all weekend and every day until we're done," he said. "We've got 100 people on the job right now in the rain, pulling off the rest of the roof with cranes, trying to get back into the dry. We didn't waste any time."[35]

Those first few days at the Rec Center were chaotic. It felt like the first day of school all over again. We attended an orientation of sorts where we received our new schedules. They were essentially the same, but due to the teachers traveling back and forth between the high school and the Bill Harmon Center, some of the class times changed. The basketball gym and meeting rooms were converted into classrooms with makeshift walls and rolling whiteboards. We had to quickly learn our new rooms and rely on the teachers to dismiss us on time since there was no bell system to alert us to move between classes. Every morning, breakfast was provided for us. Lunch was also available, but students with cars and good grades could sign out to eat elsewhere.

After being out of school for a week because of the damage a tornado wreaked havoc upon the school, students returned to class on Thursday,

April 9.

That very day, weather forecasters were calling for severe storms so administrators, teachers and students were a bit anxious. At about 11:00 the Pulaski County weather sirens began to blare and squeals were heard echoing in the hallways as students began realizing what they were hearing. Students were then moved from the trailers, the V-building, and the main building classrooms to the downstairs hallway.

Current storm information was given to the teachers who passed it on to students. Everyone was relieved that there had been no tornado sightings and that the affected area was a different part of Pulaski County. Everyone sat quietly for just over 30 minutes until the area was released from the warning. At that time students were released to 1st lunch/4th period.

While in the hallways, students and teachers used the time to discuss the emergency preparedness plan of the school. Many said that it was good that we had taken cover, if only as practice for any future tornado threats from tornados.

Several students asked why SHHS doesn't have monthly tornado drills. Assistant principal Mr. Gene Adams said, "We are going to have some tornado drills now so that when and if we have another tornado everyone will know exactly what to do." [36]

"The parents and the community will be very, very happy with the effort that all of us are making here to take care of the kids and not drag our feet," Ebbs told district and city leaders. *"I'll make sure that in Sylvan Hills and Sherwood, that gets out."*[31]

"Things are going well. We're getting in all academics and the time for them," Ebbs said. *"It has taken a lot of cooperation, coordination and support of a lot of people to pull this off—the city of Sherwood, the police, the school . . . There are enough classrooms, though a few classeshave had to double up wherever possible. The school is concentrating on the core curriculum, the courses that seniors need to graduate this May. Electives are on hold, for now . . . I hope that we'll be back in three weeks. Our fingers are crossed,"* the principal said.[37]

On thr baseball front, with the field destroyed and reconstruction efforts nowhere in sight, we had to find inventive ways to stay prepared. The indoor facility became our home field, but it wasn't big enough to do everything we needed. If the cages were lowered, then there were six smaller areas to hit BB or soft toss. More if we hit into both side of the net. Tack on two wooden mounds salvaged from storage for bullpen sessions and the space left was only large enough to do band or weighted ball workouts. When the cages were raised, we could use the turf to take ground balls or run sprints, but it still wasn't conducive for a full practice. Each option left about twenty of us, more when the ninth graders were there, either standing around waiting for our turn or utilizing the only other large enough space, the parking lot.

All of the fields still had debris on them from the tornado, and the rest of the area around the indoor was forested, so without driving somewhere else, the parking lot was the only option left. The first time we went out, it almost felt like a joke that Coach was playing on us. The lot had a pretty large slope, there were cracks in the asphalt, and rocks surrounded the whole area. We threw or kicked as many loose rocks away as we could. First and second base were set up toward the top of the hill with third and home paced off toward the bottom. It wasn't an exact distance, but it was close enough to work with.

Coach brought out a bucket of waterlogged balls that we had collected after the storm, and we began. It took Coach a few rounds to get the hang of hitting off the asphalt. With his fungo, it wasn't hard for him to smoke one without meaning to. Every ball to third base drifted to my right after the bounce. We got plenty of practice backhanding the ball. Bunt drills and bare-handed slow rollers led to scraped knuckles or falls. A high-chopped ball had to be fielded before the second bounce, or else we'd end up with a rocket sailing past our faces. Throwing to first and second was a completely different story. The uphill toss meant a lot of low balls around the knees or skips that needed to be picked, adding another layer of difficulty. Blake got a lot of work scooping some rough hops. We tore up multiple buckets of baseballs out there. We had to be careful to leave the good ones for the cages and grab the worst ones for infield practice.

Daulton took one off the face—a bloody lip. It was the first real injury on the lot, though there would be a bunch more. If you weren't taking a ball off the bat to the leg, chest, or face, a throw from a 5-4-3 double-play ball around the horn could do it, too. Add in some rain, and we'd be lucky to get five ground balls in before someone took a spill. Fly balls were tracked down through the trees. A mishit ball meant jumping over basketball-sized rocks to make the catch. We probably should have been wearing helmets and knee pads. It was a mess, but it was all we really had without making a road trip. So, we made do. We learned the ins and outs of the parking lot in hopes that it could translate to the game field.

Since the team had no home field to practice on now, they utilized a parking lot next to the field. Foor was asked what type of drills were utilized in the parking lot as players exchanged their steel cleats for tennis shoes.

"Portable P.E. bases were laid out in the parking lot to stimulate a field as we worked on situation coverages. The most difficult part of being on this parking lot was when players had to throw over or around equipment.

Our infield drills done on black top were usually coordinated by Coach Tipton. The drills included one-on-one short hop drills, forehand and backhand. Double plays were practiced with flat gloves with a coach rolling the ball to start the play. Another drill took place when regular ground balls were hit. As time went on, the players became used to the surface and where the bad hops were located."

Outfield drills were coordinated on the black top by Coach Foor. One was when a coach threw a ball over the outfielder's left or right shoulder. The players worked on flipping their hips and running to a spot. Two separate lines were formed about 30 yards apart. With the coach standing in the middle, a ball was thrown somewhere between the players. The lead player in each line would go hard to the ball until one was called off. We also labeled one of the lines centerfielders so they could take control. Fly balls were hit over a short distance, using a fungo bat. The only area to do this was in the air through a narrow alley in the parking lot between rows of trees.

Foor said the team was limited with the amount of space they had to warm up.

"Some players had to throw around trees and large rocks. The whole team was limited on the distance they could throw. We also couldn't practive on the asphalt when it was wet because it became too slippery. When wet, the parking lot was as slick as ice. There was a lot of slipping and straining of muscles at first. Fortunately, we didn't have players sustain injuries by falling hard on the asphalt. Our players only practiced in steel cleats on real baseball fields maybe six times."[32]

Even with the challenges of practicing on a parking lot, we made the most of the space. In addition to the drills mentioned by Foor, we also worked on hitting. The indoor facility, the softball fields, and occasionally a trip to Central High School or Jackonville's Dupree park allowed us that chance to swing in the open air and work on our timing. But we didn't get much live action.

To compensate for the inconsistent live pitching, we had to adjust our approach at the plate, shorten our swings and focus on making solid contact rather than trying to crush every pitch. The emphasis was on hitting the ball where it was pitched. This approach not only helped us make better contact, but we hoped it would translate to real game situations.

Despite the limitations of our makeshift practice field, our team was able to maintain a high level of intensity and focus. We knew that every practice was an opportunity to improve, and we approached each session with a sense of purpose and determination. We had to stay sharp and hone our skills even in the absence of a proper field. We didn't know if our experience practicing on the parking lot would be worth the bumps and bruises. If nothing else, we learned to adapt to more challenging circumstance and push ourselves to new heights.

"It seems that about the only thing that can derail the powerful Sylvan Hills Baseball team might be Mother Nature herself.

Last Thursday's storms did extensive damage to Sylvan Hills High School, and also wrecked most of the Sherwood Parks athletic complex. Kevin McReynolds Field, which serves as the home field for the 15-4 (6-0 in the 6A-East Conference) Bears, was virtually ripped to shreds.

Bill Blackwood Field, home of the football/ soccer Bears, did not receive near as much damage, but snapped light poles mean that the Bears and Lady Bears soccer teams will play the remainder of their seasons on the road.

Sylvan Hills athletic director and head baseball coach Denny Tipton said he believed the girls softball field will be useable by the end of the month, but for his own team, he said there is really only one option.

*"We're going to be **road warriors**," Tipton said. "We will have to play the rest of our games on the road. Anytime you don't have a place to practice, it's a concern how much it will hurt you in the long haul."*

The Bears started the '08 conference season on a tear, outscoring their 6A-East opponents 78-9 over the first six games.

Sylvan Hills used the practice field at Little Rock Central on Monday to prepare for a critical match-up with co-leading Marion yesterday.

"It's not very good timing," Tipton said. "But we're the top two teams in the conference right now, so it's a huge pair of games for both teams. Central called and offered their field to practice on. Everyone has been really helpful.

"We've had a lot of tragedy with everything

that has been thrown at us this year, but we're going to work harder and not make any excuses."

Former Bears player Taylor Roark was killed in a car accident earlier this year.

Tipton said that around $8,000 worth of the school's baseball equipment was damaged during the storm.

The schedule remains tentative, but Tipton said the home game against Jacksonville will be moved to Dupree Park, adding he also hoped to move the scheduled April 21 home game against Searcy to nearby Dupree as well.[38]

CHAPTER 7

My senior season wasn't going as planned. With the halfway point approaching, I had a lot on my mind. One major concern was my college choice. Family, friends, and even strangers were all asking me the same question, and I was starting to feel the pressure of life after high school. While I was making visits, there was still no clarity on where I wanted to go.

The first baseball showcase I attended was at Ouachita Baptist University in the Fall. Unfortunately, it rained, so we had to stay inside. Although I performed well, the school was a small DII in the middle of nowhere, and I felt I had plenty of time to prove myself in the coming year to go to a DI university. While the campus was beautiful, everyone was friendly, and I scored well across the board, I had my eyes set on bigger things. Additionally, it was an expensive school, and although I received some academic scholarship money, I wanted to avoid student loans, so it didn't seem to be a good fit.

The next showcase was at the University of Central Arkansas. This event felt more like a baseball camp, with various hitting drills and stations to evaluate performance. Again, the weather wasn't great, so we had to stay inside their indoor facility for the entire event. The UCA coach critiqued my hand position with my bat laid flat, which resembled Albert Pujols's stance. Coach Bromley and I had worked on hitting from that position to have a quicker swing the previous summer, but I don't think they were fans of the approach. However, I was able to launch wiffleballs and basketballs off the roof while I watched others roll over ground balls.

Missouri State University offered me an academic full

ride, but the distance from Sherwood was more than I wanted. We drove around their campus after visiting my grandpa in Branson, but I never spoke with the baseball coach. We also visited the University of Arkansas in Fayetteville, where we met with several admissions counselors to discuss a potential scholarship plan. However, baseball was not discussed during these meetings.

Next, we visited Arkansas State University, where I blasted the three pitches they gave me into the outfield. Unfortunately, it rained again, so everything moved quickly, and I didn't get any traction from the coaching staff. Harding was another option, but it was another DII school, and a very strict one at that. While their coaches were interested, speaking with current players revealed strict rules, such as not being able to walk on the same side of the street as the opposite sex and needing permission from the Dean to leave campus on the weekends. None of that sounded appealing.

Despite some challenges, my dad continued taking me to universities. Arkansas Tech held a baseball camp similar to UCA, but it was another terribly rainy day, so we had to hit and do drills in the cages. I failed to receive the interest I was hoping for. We made a weekend trip up to Williams Baptist University in Walnut Ridge. Dad almost missed the right turn at the bean field. They offered me a scholarship, and someone I knew from church who was attending, so it was worth checking out. The showcase was a bit longer with more drill and very running intensive. When they told me I completed one of their shuffle drills in the fastest time they had seen, I started to become suspicious of the program. The coach was ecstatic and happy to work with me and the school to fill the remaining scholarship money to attend. However, when one of the current baseball players made a comment that only athletes and the people who were made fun of in high school attended Williams, I completely shut them down.

When we made the trip to Arkadelphia to visit Ouachita, we failed to stop by Henderson, another DII school in the same small town. Taylor chose Henderson, so I knew it was a good program. I wasn't convinced it was where I wanted to be, but I was invited by their assistant baseball coach, who coached the Russellville AAA American Legion team that I played against the previous summer. Something had impressed him enough to make the call, but when I arrived, he was off-campus. Dad and I met with Henderson's head coach without him. After the conversation finished, I had a horrible feeling about things. The coach never made eye contact, and overall, just didn't seem interested in adding me to his roster. The trip was disappointing, but Dad wasn't convinced the trip was over. He suggested that we drive across the street to Ouachita to see if their coaches were still recruiting. My performance at the showcase earlier in the year was good, but I never heard anything about a position. Their coaches were at their fieldhouse. In fact, they remembered who I was, but their scholarship roster was filled. As the conversation was winding down, one of the assistants went back into the office and brought out a walk-on form. He handed it to me and said that if I was able to attend, they would have me on the team. Afterwards, Dad and I went back to the main campus, where we ran into Mrs. Terry Peeples, a family friend. I told her that I had not made a college decision, but Ouachita was growing on me since DI baseball wasn't going to be an option that late in the Spring. Finances were the main concern. She said she would be happy to see what was available but not to get my hopes up. We thanked her and left.

The last college I visited was College of the Ozarks in Clarksville, Arkansas, now University of the Ozarks, a Division III school without baseball scholarships. The coach was interested and laid out a plan to help me pay for school. I had an academic scholarship that would cover half of the tuition, and the rest could be covered through a work-study job. It was a far cry from my original hopes, but I strongly considered the offer. When we arrived back home from the trip, there was a letter in the mail from Ouachita. The school was offering the one and only Presidential Scholarship from the School of Education that fully covered the school's tuition, room, and board. Because of lots of prayer, seeking, and timing, God and Mrs. Peeples did the impossible. I would head to DII Ouachita in the fall and walk-on the baseball team.

Sunday, April 6th, 2008

Given that the Bears were talented to begin with - starting with senior outfielder/pitcher Hunter Miller - it's unfair to say the Abundant Life transfers have turned Sylvan Hills into a contender. That's especially true considering Treece has missed most of the season with a broken hand.

But Chamber and Baxendale have contributed, with the latter emerging as the staff ace.

"It gives you depth," Tipton said. "Usually, you're going to have some kid get an injury. If we lose a Hunter Miller or a D.J. Baxendale we're still going to be OK."

Battle tested.

It's not the largest classification, but it might be the best. Team for team, it's hard to find a tougher place to play than Class 6A. Defending champion Texerkana began the season ranked nationally by Baseball America, traditional powerhouses Sylvan Hills and Watson Chapel have started strong and Marion held an undefeated record in 6A-East play before falling to Sylvan Hills on Wednesday. [39]

The headlines were filled with confusion and intrigue. How would the Sylvan Hills Bears respond? We held a record of 15-4 overall and were 6-0 in the 6A-East Conference. Over those six games, we outscored our conference opponents 78-9. However, with no field to practice on and two conference games against the Marion Patriots, who were also 6-0 in the conference, coming up in a few days, everyone was curious to know how we were going to match up. Our transition from practicing on the parking lot to playing on a real baseball field would be tested quickly.

Marion Coach Mac Hurley badly wanted to take at least one victory from 6A leader Sylvan Hills last week. It didn't happen. Our team was shaky during our first game back in action, struggling to adjust to the different playing conditions. The balls bounced differently, the grass was not the same, and there were no rocks to trip over. But, as the game went on, we slowly found our rhythm, and by the end, we had won in a close battle, 2-1.

Sylvan Hills swept Marion Tuesday, winning 2 - 1 and 7 - 1. But Marion still has a good shot at a second-place conference finish. That sits well with Hurley, seeing as how the top two teams in each 6A conference get a first-round bye in the State Tournament. Playing three games instead of two can mean a world difference when it comes to managing a pitching staff.[40]

Using the parking lot as a practice field just became one of the many obstacles we had to adapt to and overcome. Through our resourcefulness and determination, we made the most of our limited resources and turned them into a winning formula. With hard work, dedication, and a little creativity, anything became possible, and Marion found out the hard way.

Overall Arkansas School Records
1. Fayetteville 18 - 1.
2. Bryant 11 - 2
3. Benton 16 - 3
4. Sylvan Hills 15 - 4
5. Bentonville 11 - 7
6. Texarkana 15 - 7

Class 6A
1. Benton 16 - 3
2. Sylvan Hills 15 -4
3. Texarkana 15 - 7[40]

Our team's success wasn't limited to the field. We overcame plenty of challenges off the field, too. The aftermath of the tornado left the community in shambles, and many families were still struggling to rebuild homes and businesses. The team and school rallied together and organized several opportunities to help those in need. We worked to clear debris, distribute food and water, and assist with the rebuilding efforts.

Tuesday, April 15, 2008
Sylvan Hills @ Forrest City Mustangs
Conference Doubleheader

With West Memphis and Marion behind us, our focus shifted to Forrest City. We traveled east on Interstate-40 towards Memphis to face the Mustangs, who held a 9-7 overall record and a 3-3 conference record. Their offense had struggled, but their pitching kept them in most games. Before we left the indoor facility, Coach Tipton and Foor discussed strategy to overcome their pitching duo, Justin Cochran and Barrett Astin.

Instead of starting D.J. as usual, the plan was to pit him against Astin regardless of which game Astin started, and have Hunter start against Cochran. The doubleheader could become a pitching duel, so the hope was that our pitching could outplay theirs. As we warmed up and learned that Hunter was starting the first game, the atmosphere shifted. Perhaps it was the drive, the relatively empty stands, or the field's Little League feel that affected us.

Until this series, D.J. had started every game, dominating our opponents and limiting them to under three runs per outing. In the four conference games he started, we outscored our rivals 49-4. Watching Hunter take the mound first, despite being our number two pitcher, had an unexpected impact. Hunter's games, on the other hand, were not bad but had resulted in a 38-7 scoreline in our favor. One would not think that starting Hunter in the first game would make a significant difference, but it did. For some inexplicable reason, we weren't as sharp to start the game.

> *Forrest City senior Justin Cochran got the start for the Mustangs in the first game and came up big by going the distance to earn the 7-1 victory. Cochran worked seven full innings, giving up one run on one hit and four walks while striking out five Bears and hitting one Sylvan Hills' batter.*
>
> *His counterpart, Sylvan Hills pitcher Hunter Miller failed to match the success he enjoyed as the starting quarterback for the Sylvan Hills football team, lasting only 2-1/3 innings,*

giving up six runs on six hits with three strikeouts. Miller also committed two errors in the crucial third inning which helped jump start the Mustang offensive uprising.

Daulton gave up one run on two hits and one walk in his three and 2/3 innings of work.

Cochran made the 7-1 lead stand up, allowing only two Sylvan Hills base runners over the final four innings, both by walks and leaving both stranded at first base.[41]

Our hearts sank as the game ended, marking our first conference loss of the season and breaking a thirteen-game winning streak that dated back a month. A single hit in a seven-inning game was a rude awakening. We were not invincible, and our destroyed fields, perfect conference record, and dominant performances thus far meant nothing to the Forrest City Mustangs who stole a win. They earned it, and we tipped our hats to them.

Before the start of the second game, Coach Tipton held a quick meeting. He was not just angry; he was furious. He knew we were better than the way we played in the first game. Our one-hit baseball reminded him of our early season struggles, not our mid-season triumphs. We needed a wake-up call, and we got one in the first inning of Game 2.

Game two began with quite a bang when Sylvan Hills head coach Denny Tipton was ejected in the first inning after arguing a "bang-bang" call at first base.[41]

The play at first was a close call, but it was hard to see from the third base dugout if it was the right call. However, it was the umpire changing his decision after intervention from Forrest City's coach that set Tipton off. There had been a few rough ones in the first game, but nothing quite like this. Coach charged across the field, and a shouting match ensued. They went back and forth pointing at the base and shoe print in the dirt, then back to the base, until finally, the umpire yelled, *"You're gone!"*

Coach Tipton exchanged a few more words before storming off to the dugout, leaving Coach Foor frantic, trying to figure out how to lead the team. Quick plans were made while the home plate umpire yelled at Coach Tipton to leave. He grabbed his bag and headed to a building behind the left field fence to pace while we turned our attention back to the game. We were fired up. This was what we needed to jump start us. The dynamics had changed.

> *Tipton's outburst and ejection woke the Bears from their one game hibernation . . . Sylvan Hills plated three runs in the bottom of the first inning using two walks, one sacrifice and one hit batter, as Clint Thornton, Miller and Eller all scored. Sylvan Hills got runs from Eller and Justin Treece in the bottom of the third to push the lead to 5-0 before the Mustangs got on the board in the top of the fourth when Laws singled, went to second on a passed ball and scored when Patillo's ground ball was misplayed for an error. The Bears added a pair of runs in the sixth inning when*

Miller and D.J. Baxendale had consecutive singles and each scored.

That would be all the Mustangs would get in the nightcap as starting junior pitcher Baxendale went the distance, holding the Mustangs to the one run while scattering five hits with one walk and recording nine strikeouts.

Make no mistake, Sylvan Hills has proved to be the best baseball team in the 6A-East Conference, and will more than likely win the outright league championship. The Bears have displayed superhuman tendencies through the first eight conference games, going unbeaten and outscoring their opponents by more than three to one.

But Tuesday at Forrest City, their mortality showed for the first time this season and the Mustangs took full advantage of the suddenly "human" Bears by going where no other team in the 6A-East has been this season.

Forrest City entered Tuesday's conference varsity doubleheader with visions of winning both ends of the twin bill. They settled for a split, and for the moment own the title of being the only 6A-East team with a victory over the Bears.

The Mustangs won the opening game 7-1, before Sylvan Hills regained their league-leading form and took game two by the identical 7-1 score. The Bears stand at 9-1 in the conference while the Mustangs are 4-4 in the East and 9-7 overall.

The doubleheader had everything a baseball fan could want — a huge pitching performance by one of the smallest players on the field, a one-inning meltdown, a one-inning offensive outburst, a meltdown and ejection of a head coach and enough hit batters to last an entire season.

The Class 6A State Tournament begins May 9 at Texarkana. The 6A-East conference will send the top six teams to the tournament to face the top six teams from the 6A-South conference.[41]

Saturday, April 19th, 2008
Sylvan Hills @ Fayetteville Bulldogs
Non-Conferene Opponent

I remember Coach Tipton asking me before we got on the bus if my Dad was driving up to Fayetteville for the game. Dad never wanted to miss me playing. He stepped in to coach my little league teams growing up and had hardly missed since. However, with me getting little playing time, the game being three hours away, and after the situation at Conway, I figured I wasn't playing, and he wasn't coming. I called to ask him what he was planning on doing. He said exactly what I thought, that if I wasn't playing, he wasn't driving up. I relayed the message to Coach and went back to my routine.

Coach came back and told me to let my Dad know that I'd be starting at third base against Fayetteville. I couldn't believe it. It didn't seem real because I hadn't seen the field in several weeks. It made sense that Coach would give some of the starters a break leading into the last four conference games and the tournament. None of that mattered to me at the time. I was just excited to play. I called Dad, and he said he would come.

It was a Saturday trip on a hot day, one of the few non-rainy days we had over the month. Fayetteville was on a tear. They were two-time defending State Champions, earning one in 5A in 2006 before the shift to the 6A system and then in 6A in 2007 before the switch to the 7A system this year. The last team to win the class with Fayetteville in it was 5A Sylvan Hills in 2005. Our rival was on a school-record twenty-two game winning streak. That's the environment we were walking into.

We got to the game, warmed up, and headed back to the dugout. Coach Foor called on the lineup. I kept waiting to hear my name. One after another, it wasn't there. I was expected to bat seventh, eighth, or ninth, but I didn't hear my name in the lineup at all. Coach finished reading it off, then said I was playing third, and they were DHing Nathan for me.

I wanted to leave. If my Dad had been there at this point, I probably would have asked to go home with him. I called really quick to see if he was close to let him know not to come, but he was around the corner. The disappointment in his voice was apparent, and I'm sure he heard mine. I guess I was considered a liability in the batter's box or on the basepaths.

We took the field for the bottom of the first, and I don't remember much else of what happened. The only play that sticks out was a line drive to me at third base that I never saw. It came so hard that I only had time to throw my glove up in reaction. The ball bounced off my palm and fell to the ground. The runner had already retreated to first thinking it was a catch, so I made a quick throw to second for an out. Clint's relay to first wasn't in time for the double play. One out. No harm done. Even if I caught the ball clean, the runner wouldn't have advanced.

The Bulldogs won 3-1, leaving ten runners stranded on the bases. Our only run was scored in the fifth inning, following a double from Jake and a ground ball hit by Spears to second base.

> *"Most of our nonconference games are against 7A competition and this was good for us," Sylvan Hills coach Denny Tipton said. "We knew Fayetteville was obviously going to be a good baseball team. We knew it would be a good test for us but we can't expect to beat good teams with only three hits. We hit the ball hard and didn't strike out but I don't think we swung the bats well until the fourth inning. We had some good at-bats but we needed more hits."* [42]

Monday, April 21, 2008
Searcy Lions @ Sylvan Hills
Conference Doubleheader

> *The first game began as a close one and turned into a rout. The second one began as a rout, turned into a close one and finished with a flourish.*
>
> *Both were Sylvan Hills wins. The Bears improved to 11-1 in the 6A-East and 22-6 overall with a dramatic seventh-inning rally to beat*

Searcy 12-9 in Game 2 of a doubleheader on Monday at Dupree Park. In the first game, it was all Sylvan Hills from the second inning on in a 12-0, five-inning affair.

"We go as our bats go," said Sylvan Hills head coach Denny Tipton. "Our pitching and our defense have been pretty good all year. We either get two hits or 10 hits. That's kind of the way it's gone all year."

Baxendale tossed a three-hitter in the opener, and while he wasn't overpowering — at least by the standards he's set this season — he was plenty good enough. He allowed three hits over the first two innings, then pitched hitless ball over the final three. He struck out four and walked two.

"I didn't think D.J. threw as well as he's been throwing," Tipton said. "But he's come off a couple of 100-pitch outings and we were hoping to get out of here with 75. We'd have probably pulled him if he'd reached that. [Baxendale threw only 66 pitches]. We know it's a long year."

His counterpart, Searcy hurler Anthony Dillon, [sat] down the Bears in order in the first before Baxendale's single, Chambers' double and Justin Treece's single in the second put Sylvan Hills up 2-0. The Bears missed an opportunity to blow it open in the third when they left the bases loaded.

But they began to get to Dillon in the

fourth, when they scored three more runs. Treece doubled leading off, and Spears singled. Evans sent a sharp single to right to score Treece, then came across on Mark Turpin's double off the top of the fence in left. Miller's bloop single over the second baseman scored Turpin to make it 5-0.

Evans delivered a two-run single in the fifth, when Sylvan Hills put the game away. Thornton drove in another with a long sacrifice fly to right, and Miller ended it with his 10th home run of the season — a towering three-run blast to left. Miller had four RBI in the contest to go along with three for Evans and two for Treece. Sylvan Hills had 13 hits — two each by Miller, Chambers, Treece and Evans.

"It was nice to have a few fall for us today," *Tipton said. "Searcy is always a good club."* [62]

And with the win in the second game, we secured our third conference championship in a row. The last two conference games would be a formality as our number one seed could not be challenged. But that would not stop us from wanting to finish the season strong. Only a few more games before the tournament. There was no reason to let off the gas.

Denny Tipton encourages his batters to keep their swings as compact as possible. But there is one player the Sylvan Hills head baseball coach is willing to grant a little license to in the matter of batting strokes.

When Hunter Miller's typically aggressive swing resulted in a towering game-ending shot over the fence in left against Searcy last Tuesday, Tipton wasn't inclined to tell Miller to shorten it up. After all, it was Miller's 10th round-tripper of the season.

He's batting .397 with 32 RBI and 39 runs in just 28 games. In other words, if it isn't broke ...

"We work hard on keeping swings a little shorter," said Tipton, whose Bears just clinched the 6A-East title with a sweep of Searcy and are 22-6 overall. "But Hunter's always going to be naturally long. To me, he's just a natural hitter."

Tipton said Miller actually has made some improvements in his swing over the past three years. Used to be, Tipton said, Miller would hit towering fly balls that would be caught 10 feet short of the fence. Now, he gets on top of the ball better. The result:

Ten home runs this year to go along with eight his junior season. He hit only one as a sophomore.

Miller doesn't particularly look like a power hitter. But Tipton said his bat speed, explosiveness and leverage help offset any brawn deficiency he may suffer from.

"I take my hacks when I get up to the plate," *Miller said. "I don't go up there looking for walks. I'm up there swinging the bat. That's just how I am. This is the most athletic team I've played on since I've been here," said Miller, who saw some action as a freshman and has started all three years since then. "We can compete with anybody in the state. It would be very disappointing [if we don't reach the championship game] because we have every player in the book we need to win it. So we think we should get there and win it."*

Tipton knows he's got a loaded club, but he isn't as willing as Miller to turn this into an all-or-nothing season. Winning the conference is always the No. 1 goal, he said. After that, it's to win one game at a time in the state tournament.

"Is [getting to the championship game] what we expect?" Tipton asks. "Yes. I'd be lying to people if I didn't say that. But there are some good teams out there and only two teams ever make it. If we take care of ourselves, I think we've got a good shot."[63]

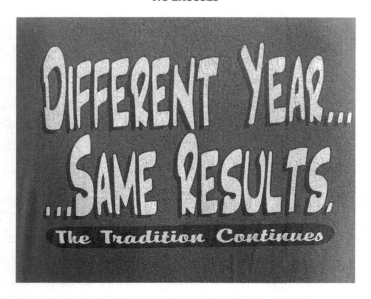

Wednesday, April 30, 2008
Sylvan Hills @ Jacksonville Red Devils
Conference Doubleheader

Our final two conference games were against Jacksonville. As far as tournament seeding was concerned, we were guaranteed to keep our number one seed in the East regardless of how these games ended. The Red Devils were also securely in the tournament, but they had a game and a half remaining against West Memphis that had been postponed due to rain. Depending on how their last four games went, they could end up anywhere between the fourth and sixth seed. We didn't want to add any more losses to our conference record after the Forrest City trip, and since we had already lost to Jacksonville earlier in the season, we were determined to get payback.

The Red Devils got off to a good start in the opener against Sylvan Hills ace D.J. Baxendale when, with two outs, Hood singled and Castleberry homered to left. Baxendale settled down after that, retiring the next 13 Jacksonville batters.

That gave the Bears' offense plenty of time to mount a comeback. They tied it in the second on Chambers' RBI single and a double steal. Miller gave them a 4-2 lead by following Mark Turpin's leadoff single in the third with his 11th home run of the season. The Bears put it away by scoring five runs on just one hit in the fifth and sixth innings. But that hit was a big one — a three-run shot by Thornton over the fence in left-center that made it 7-2.

The Red Devils loaded the bases with no outs in the sixth on a walk to Noah Sanders, Terrell Brown's single and an error. Hood grounded into a force at third that allowed Sanders to score, and Regnas came around on the play when Eller's throw to first was wild. But Ellers made up for it by starting a sterling 5-4-3 double play to end the game in the seventh. Tyler Wisdom took the loss for Jacksonville, allowing five hits, three walks and four earned runs over 2 1/3 innings. Baxendale went the distance for the Bears, allowing four hits and a walk, while fanning eight.

Sylvan Hills' Hunter Miller out-dueled Michael Harmon to complete the sweep with a 3-0 win in the nightcap after the Bears shook off the pesky Red Devils, 9-4, in the opener. Not that the Red Devils were happy to lose two, but the performance they got on the mound from Harmon in the nightcap gives Burrows plenty of reason for optimism as they prepare for state tournament play next week.

Harmon tossed a five-hitter and carried a two-hit shutout into the sixth inning before D.J. Baxendale lined a sharp single to left to score Hunter Miller and break the scoreless tie. The Bears added a pair of insurance runs in the nightcap on Wednesday when Jordan Spears lined *a single to right and moved to second on Tyler Van Schuyck's bunt single. Spears eventually scored on Clint Thornton's sacrifice fly, while Van Schuyck plated the final run on a wild pitch.*

As good as Harmon was, Miller was just a little better, allowing three hits through six innings before Nathan Ellers closed it out with a 1-2-3 seventh. "Harmon threw a great game," said Sylvan Hills coach Denny Tipton. "We didn't hit it very well, but I give him a lot of credit. Hunter pitched really well, too. That was six good, quality innings. We needed that before state." Sylvan Hills, which improved to 24-6, and finished the 6A-East 13-1, clinched the conference title last week and will take a No. 1 seed into state tournament play.[43]

To finish out the regular season, we played games against Nettleton and Whitehall. I don't remember much of either game though I did start against White Hall. Both were wins and set us up for a run in the tournament.

Parking lot powerhouse
Sylvan Hills (26-6) overcomes death, destruction

CHAPTER 8

In the week leading up to the tournament, I was physically and mentally worn out. In addition to our regular practices and tournament preparation, it was also the first week of AP exams, and I had five to take. They were administered at a local church near our high school. Each test was approximately three to four hours long, and I had very few breaks as I tried to turn my chaotic year into college credit. I had Calculus on 5/7 and European History on 5/9 in the afternoon. Then, in week two, I had Music Theory on 5/12, Chemistry on 5/13, and English Language on 5/14. All of this was happening while State Tournament games were taking place in between.

That was also the week that some of the seniors decided that the team should cut their hair into mohawks. I wasn't present for the first round, but when they showed up at the Bill

Harmon, they made a statement. It was a show of solidarity, a way to demonstrate how much of a team we were despite everything that had occurred throughout the year. Even Hunter, who had long, bushy hair, cut it and used a ponytail holder to keep it up. He had a horse mane vibe going. When I arrived at the indoor facility, the trimmers were already buzzing on one of the underclassman volunteers. McKinney jumped in the chair at some point and wanted his hair cut to resemble the seams of a baseball all around the rim of his head. When they finished, he looked like he had Caesar's laurel wreath instead. I don't think it came out the way he was hoping, but he turned it into a positive with a few laughs. The Caesar nickname stuck.

Hunter attempted to persuade me to jump in, too, but I declined. It wasn't my thing. He pushed a few times, but I wouldn't budge. At the time, I still hadn't decided which college I was attending and had several interviews set up, so I used that as an excuse for not wanting to get a mohawk. He countered, saying that it would be beneficial for my interviews as it showed team spirit. It would demonstrate that I was all in and a dedicated team player. He was correct. It would undoubtedly be a fantastic way to start a conversation. However, I still declined. I didn't want a mohawk, and honestly, I didn't feel connected to the team. It had been that way for weeks. I felt like an afterthought, and my investment level in the team was at a four-year low. In my mind, I had more important things to prepare for, such as college, church, or relationships. I knew I probably wouldn't see the field in the tournament, so why should I give more to the team? However, I did compromise by creating a faux-hawk with some gel. That was as close as I would get to cutting my hair.

I'm fairly certain that was the same day Coach bought all of us $5 Hot 'N Ready pizzas from Little Caesars. Everyone got an entire pizza to themselves. Perez and I sat indoors and ate every last bite. I don't know why that memory stuck in my mind. Coach regularly took us out to eat before and after games, whether it was stopping at Wendy's on the way out of town or making a fancier visit to Ryan's where we could eat unlimited steak, and the buffet was nearly empty.

When Coach Tipton saw everyone's hair, he was

surprised, but he went along with it. There wasn't much he could do at this point. He did inform us that one of the local news stations would be coming to film a segment on the "Road Warriors" in the next few days. Of course, the team decided to go hatless to display our haircuts. We were filmed hitting in the indoor, and, of course, taking ground balls off the asphalt lot.

>   *Clint Thornton has his eyes fixed off in the distance as his voice starts to fade. "I don't know what to say," said Thornton, a senior second baseman/right fielder at Sylvan Hills. "Just emotionally, we've been through so much." He pauses. "This is the best team I've played for."*

>   *It's hard to pinpoint when the 2008 Sylvan Hills Bears should have gone off the track. It could have been when the influx of transfers nabbed the playing time of some of the team's experienced players.*

>   *Or it could have been Jan. 25, when 2007 Sylvan Hills graduate and former teammate and captain Taylor Roark was killed in a two-car accident.*

>   *Then there were the storms of April 3, which left the team without a field and one of its players without a home.*

>   *Yet here they are, sitting at 26-6 with the No. 1 seed out of the 6A-East for the Class 6A State Tournament, which begins today in Texarkana.*

>   *Say this about the Bears: They're not likely*

to be rattled by anything that happens on the field.

"Outside of playing baseball, this team has been through a lot," Sylvan Hills Coach Denny Tipton said.

As Tipton said this, the Bears were taking warm-up tosses on the concrete parking lot that passes for their practice field. The storms and high winds that hit the metro area early last month were especially cruel to the Sherwood school, damaging its high school campus and all but destroying its baseball field.

Since then, the Bears have played their remaining schedule on the road, winning all but two games - one loss to Class 7A Fayetteville and the other to Forrest City. Rather than scavenge for places to practice, Sylvan Hills has mostly made do with its indoor batting cages and the occasional dicey infield session on the parking lot.

Tipton estimates the Bears have maybe practiced on a real field three times since April 3.

"We kind of got a little rusty," Thornton said. "We played worse than we were, but we still managed to get our wins. We're getting it, though. We started playing a little better last week."

Not that anyone's complaining. It's hard for Thornton to whine when he sees senior catcher J.T. Long bounding into practice with the same enthusiasm he had before he lost his home.

Long was at his house on Loop Road, near

the school's baseball complex, April 3 when the high winds hit. He took shelter with the rest of his family inside a closet, only to walk outside and find the closet was one of the few things left standing.

"We went outside and everything was just destroyed," Long said. "Our gas alarm was going off because we were leaking gas."

Long and his family spent the rest of the rainy night picking through their belongings with help from Tipton, senior pitcher Hunter Miller and other team members. "I miss my bed, for one," said Long, whose family is living with his grandparents nearby. "It was an ultra king size."

The storms hit just as the team was beginning to recover from the death of Roark, who was about halfway through his freshman year at Henderson State when his truck hit a patch of ice on Interstate 30 near the Clark-Hot Springs county line and collided with a tractor trailer.

"It was one of the hardest things I've dealt with in my coaching career," said Tipton, in his 11th year coaching the Bears. "If you knew Taylor, he was just so well-liked."

As the Bears started baseball practice under the cloud of Roark's death, the team's veterans had another issue to handle. Three players from nearby Abundant Life - shortstop Justin Treece, outfielder Jake Chambers and pitcher D.J. Baxendale - opted to transfer to Sylvan Hills when

Wes Johnson, their coach at Abundant Life, left the school to take a job as a volunteer assistant at Central Arkansas. Joined by another transfer, Vilonia's Chris Perez, the newcomers made for a talented foursome that pushed some returning players into reduced roles. Baxendale is now one of the Bears' two conference starters, Chambers has worked his way into the lineup and Treece has become a contributor after breaking a hand earlier in the season. Perez, meanwhile, is 3-0, including a victory over 7A Central champ Little Rock Catholic.

"It put a lot of stress on everybody else," Thornton said. "We didn't know who any of them were, we just knew they were some good ballplayers."

And that ultimately helped them get accepted. "Me and Jake, we knew most of these kids growing up," Treece said. "D.J. probably had it the toughest because he came from Arkadelphia [before moving to Abundant Life as a sophomore.] Everybody's just taken us in as if we've been here since ninth grade."

Given all that's happened since January, it's no wonder some of the Bears have taken to wearing shirts under their uniforms with the slogan "No Excuses." It's also no wonder that most of them are saying the 2008 baseball season won't be soon forgotten no matter what happens in the State Tournament.

"All this stuff has brought us closer together," Treece said. *"It doesn't matter what happens, we're going to pull through and do it. Everybody on this team, we're like brothers."*[44]

Favorite game of the season?

"The North Little Rock game made us realize we needed to play smarter. I liked the lollipop play, because it wass always unexpected."

Blake Rix
senior

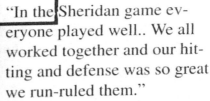

"In the Sheridan game everyone played well.. We all worked together and our hitting and defense was so great we run-ruled them."

Jake Chambers
senior

Heading into the tournament, we were the favorite from the East, but that didn't stop the pundits from bringing up the past two seasons. The 2005 Championship didn't matter after the poor performances since. Internet chat rooms and talk radio were abuzz, questioning the conference meltdown loss against Forrest City and wanting to know when the SH prom was this year. It wasn't something most of us players were aware of, but the rumors were seeping in. Jonesboro, Texarkana, and Watson Chapel were all powerhouses that received a Round 1 Tournament Bye. None could be overlooked, but neither could a dark horse team like Searcy or Jacksonville. Playing at Texarkana, which was so far away from the rest of the state, was on the minds of many teams, especially with their school seeking a second major championship on the year after football.

Every year, Coach Tipton would give us this speech about finding a balance throughout the season and peaking at the right time. If we peaked too early, then our opponents would be able to take advantage of our flailing offense or pitching, and we would lose. It was just as bad to never hit a stride and fail to peak at all. A fine balance that required us to stay focused on the present while still keeping our heads up enough to plan for the next game. Now any game could be our last, as seen in the previous years. The question became, had we peaked at the right time, or were we bound for a downward slide?

Friday, May 9th, 2008
Class 6A State Tournament @ Texarkana

FRIDAY'S GAMES

Game 1 Jacksonville vs. Sheridan, 4:00 p.m.

Game 2 Lake Hamilton vs. Searcy, 4:00 p.m.

Game 3 Benton vs. Forrest City, 6:30 p.m.

Game 4 Marion vs. El Dorado, 6:30 p.m.

SATURDAY'S GAMES

Game 5 Watson Chapel vs. Winner Game 1, noon

Game 6 Sylvan Hills vs. Winner Game 2, noon

Game 7 Jonesboro vs. Winner Game 3, 2:30 p.m.

Game 8 Texarkana vs. Winner Game 4, 2:30 p.m.[45]

Sylvan Hills will enter this weekend's 6A state tournament as the No. 1 seed out of the East after a near-flawless 13-1 run through the league schedule . . .head coach Denny Tipton said the mental toughness of his top-ranked team equals its talent.

"I think we've been through a lot this year," Tipton said. "From what happened with Taylor Roark at the first of the year, to the tornados, to people getting hurt, we've had to fight through so much. These kids are very tough mentally, and I think they will be prepared. Physically, I fully believe they are as tough and talented as any group we've had in the last few seasons. If they

play to the best of their abilities, we should have a shot at winning some games."

Despite the Bears' immaculate record in the 6A East, the final few games did not feature the offensive firepower of their early league romps. Tipton said clinching the top seed early, along with the nasty weather this spring, led to a few lackluster efforts during late-season outings. He's hoping that the state tourney will rekindle that early fire.

"Everyone is 0-0 now," Tipton said. "I know everybody's plan is to go all the way, and right now, everybody has the same shot everyone else does. I hope we can come out and swing our bats with a little more intensity than what we have recently.

"I know that those final games weren't very important seed-wise, but we just weren't playing with a lot of intensity. As a coach, you're never really satisfied, and there's always room to improve." [64]

Friday, May 9th, 2008
6A South Lake Hamilton Wolves
vs.
6A East Searcy Lions
Round 1 of the State Tournament
@ Texarkana

The Searcy Lions were on fire as they advanced to the quarterfinals against the Sylvan Hills Bears. Their win against Lake Hamilton Wolves had been an impressive display of offensive power, with everyone in the lineup getting at least one hit. Coach McCammon was pleased with his team's performance, and he knew that they would need to keep up their level of play if they wanted to advance further in the playoffs.

Anthony Dillon had been outstanding on the mound, pitching all seven innings and only giving up one run. His teammates had provided plenty of run support, with fourteen hits and ten runs.

> *Everyone on the lineup got a hit for Searcy, McCammon said. At the plate, Dillon Howard was 3-for-4 with an RBI. Jonathan Luthe was 2-for-3 with three RBI. Matt Ellis was 2-for-4 with three RBI, all coming on a home run. Zack Langley had a big day at the plate, as he went 2-for-4 with two RBI. Justin Drain went 1-for-4, while Dillon, Tate Ruddell, Nathan Leonard and Jordan Bradley each went 1-for-3.*
>
> *The Lions will now prepare to face a familiar opponent at noon today when they take on Sylvan Hills, a fellow member of the 6A East Conference. While both teams know the other's strengths and weaknesses, McCammon said it was important for Searcy to continue to play the best it could."* [46]
>
> *McCammon knew that this would be a tough game, but he was confident that his players*

could rise to the occasion. They had already proven that they could play at a high level, and he encouraged them to keep playing their best.

"We know Sylvan Hills has a good team," McCammon said. *"I feel like these kids are up for the challenge. If we play like we did today, then we should be OK."* [46]

The quarterfinal game against Sylvan Hills would be played at noon the next day with McCammon and his team were already preparing for the challenge. The Lions showed they were a force to be reckoned with. They were determined to continue their winning streak. With their sights set on the state championship, the Searcy Lions were ready to take on anyone who stood in their way.

Saturday, May 10th, 2008
6A East Searcy Lions
vs.
6A East Sylvan Hills Bears
Quarterfinals of the State Tournament
@ Texarkana

The Bears (26-6 overall) will begin tournament play today, facing the winner of last night's first-round game between Searcy (East No. 5) and Lake Hamilton (South No. 4). [64]

The Searcy Lions had come off an impressive win against Lake Hamilton. Despite having faced Searcy before, Coach

Tipton still wanted our team to arrive early in Texarkana to avoid any potential setbacks. Memories of the 2007 collapse still lingered, and we were determined not to let it happen again.

After spending the night in Texarkana, our team woke up early to hit in the cages at an independent baseball club's field. Cages were divided into four areas to maximize each player's swings. We needed to be warmed up and ready for the game ahead. As we practiced, some pitchers from the independent league team arrived for bullpen sessions, including a smaller Asian man who caught the attention of his coaches with a submarine pitching style.

Although some comments were made about us being able to hit their pitchers, our team knew that these players were living out their dreams of playing professional baseball. We couldn't fault them for wanting to play one more game. We finished practicing, boarded the bus with Mr. B, and headed towards Arkansas High School, where we would face off against Searcy.

The Lions' previous victory against Lake Hamilton did not translate to this game. Dillon Howard took the mound for Searcy, while Hillside's D.J. Baxendale pitched for us. We held the Lions to just three singles, and they couldn't get anything going against us, who won 5-0.

Reflecting on the season, Coach McCammon spoke positively about the team's progress. While the loss to Sylvan Hills was disappointing, the team would be ready to come back even stronger the next year.

"In Friday's game against Lake Hamilton,
I thought it was our best game of the year,"

McCammon said.

"We faced a good Sylvan Hills team Saturday. We made some great strides during the season, but we just couldn't get anything going against Sylvan Hills."[47]

Monday, May 12th, 2008
6A South Texarkana Razorbacks
vs.
6A East Sylvan Hills Bears
Semifinals of the State Tournament
@ Texarkana

Fans who attended Monday's semifinal game between Sylvan Hills and Texarkana pretty much knew in advance they would be seeing an excellent game. Texarkana has been in the championship game the last two seasons, winning one title. Sylvan Hills was busy winning championships two of the three seasons before that.

Aside from the strong tradtions of both programs, the two teams also feature two of the best players in the state. The concensus among the top half of the state is that Hunter Miller is probably the best all-around player in the state. Ask fans in the southern half of Arkansas and they'll point you in the direction of Texarkana's Bo Bigham.[48]

A scoreless first inning for both teams wouldn't last long as Spears started us off with a single in the second. Casey pinch ran for him and immediately stole second base. The gamble payed off as Ty's line drive into center would bring Casey home for our first run. Another pinch runner, this time Ryan for Ty at first, and another stolen base led to our second run as Clint doubled to right.

> It was theme for the night: Get on base and run. The Bears stole seven bases in the contest, losing only one when Mike Maddox was out at third in the fifth. They had another runner picked off.
>
> "We like to run," Tipton said. "That's our game plan every game. We hit the ball hard and ran the bases well. And we played great defense. Clint Thornton at second base made a lot of great plays."[65]

Hunter started the third inning by getting hit by the pitch and followed it by immediately stealing second base. They knew it was coming, and still Texarkana could not stop him. A line drive from Nathan to centerfield and Hunter scored our third and final run of the game. The hits and runs stopped coming, but three runs was all we needed.

> But the story of the game remained Baxendale, who [allowed] only four base runners on two hits and two walks. After issuing a pair of walks in the third, he retired 12 in a row and 13 of the final 14.
>
> The only Razorback to reach during that span was Josh Stringfellow, who was credited with a single when his pop up into shallow left with two outs

in the seventh dropped in between shortstop Justin Treece and left fielder Mark Turpin after an apparent miscommunication between the two.

But Baxendale recorded his 10th strikeout of the game to send Sylvan Hills to the state title game for the first time since 2005.

"I knew they could swing it one through eight (in their lineup)," Baxendale said. "So I had to really be focused and make sharp pitches and go after them with everything I had. I tried to keep them off guard. I've got seven or eight pitches so it was kind of hard for them to guess what pitch was coming."

Tyler Weir got Arkansas High's only other hit — a solid single to center in the first inning.

"These teenagers, with their adrenaline in the state tournament is going to carry them a lot," Tipton said of Baxendale's 11 innings of work over three days. "Texarkana swings the bat well. But D.J. has great stuff and throws from a lot of different angles. He's just a great pitcher. Once again, we're capable of hitting it all the way through the lineup," Tipton said. "I like multiple-hit games from guys. But it's a team game, and we got some hits when we needed them. It's always your goal [to get to the state championship]," he said. "But we've dealt with so much. I can't lie. I think it means something more with everything we've been through."

His heart didn't appear to be in it when he said it, but Arkansas High head coach Mike Lloyd suggested that, if his team and Sylvan Hills could play a 7-game series, it might be a different story.

Maybe Lloyd was thinking someone other than D.J. Baxendale would be pitching those games for the Bears. But with Baxendale on the mound, it's hard to imagine a much different outcome than the 3-0 shutdown D.J. and the Bears put on the Razorbacks on Monday night to advance to the 6A state championship game at Baum Stadium in Fayetteville.

"In a single-game elimination, if you come up and run into a guy that's having a good night, that's the way it can happen," Lloyd said of Baxendale's performance. "I tip my hat to him."

Baxendale, the junior transfer from Abundant Life, showed no effects from having pitched 48 hours earlier, tossing a 2-hitter against an Arkansas High team with a potent lineup. These Razorbacks are the same team that was ranked in the top 20 nationally and that features a slugger in Garrett Underwood who hit four consecutive home runs in one game this season.

Baxendale was coming off a 51-pitch, 4-inning outing against Searcy in the state quarterfinals on Saturday. Sylvan Hills head coach Denny Tipton said he realizes he took a gamble when he pulled his ace with the Bears clinging to a 2-0 lead on Saturday.

"Yeah, I probably gambled a little," said Tipton, whose club set a school record by recording its 28th win. "But it worked out."

Baxendale said he felt no fatigue on Monday. "Saturday was just like a midweek bullpen since I only threw about 50 pitches," he said. "So it didn't affect me too much. My adrenaline took over [in the seventh inning]. I knew we were three outs away, so I just reared back and went after it." [65]

D.J. Baxendale tossed a two-hit shutout against the Razorbacks after throwing four shutout innings on Saturday against Searcy. [49]

Bigham ended his season with 12 home runs and had 13 RBIs over a two game stretch in March. Miller hit his 12th home run of the season during the tournament and has a chance to show Arkansas what they missed out on this Saturday. [48]

Fans of both teams were left in awe of the incredible game they had witnessed. It was a true testament to the skill and determination and a reminder of why high school sports are such an important part of our communities.

For Texarkana, the story was over. For us, we proved we were ready to take on whatever team stood in our way in the championship game, showing again that we were one of the best high school baseball teams in the state. We were determined to add the title to our impressive record.

On the other side of the bracket, our opponent was yet to be determined. We had already made the two-hour bus ride home after our game with Searcy when I found out that Watson Chapel and Jacksonville were still playing. The game was broadcast on the radio, where it had reached the twelfth. The Red Devils, who were the number four seed from the East, had managed to pull off a come-from-behind win against Sheridan in the first round. Now, they were facing the number one seed from the South, the Wildcats.

Jacksonville's Harmon started the game and gave up two runs in the bottom of the sixth inning. Watson Chapel's early celebration was cut short by Cameron Hood and Patrick Castleberry, a couple of my old friends, getting on base, followed by a Caleb Mitchell two-run single. Harmon finished the seventh and eighth innings before bowing out due to reaching the maximum innings he could pitch. Jacksonville and Watson Chapel continued the pitching clinic, with neither team able to score until the twelfth inning.

The Red Devils unleashed a three-run barrage, assisted by a Wildcat error. While down to their last out in the bottom of the inning, the Wildcats flipped the script when Jacksonville committed a costly error, allowing a run to score, followed by two more runs that tied the game at five.

In the top of the thirteenth, Jacksonville failed to score. Chapel then set in motion a memorable series of plays. A single, a stolen second base, a wild pitch that sent the runner to third, and another single walked off the game, advancing Watson Chapel to the semifinals.

> *Watson Chapel . . . did get fortunate, surviving Jacksonville in the quarterfinals when a two-out error in the 12th inning gave them life. They rallied with three runs in the inning to tie it, then won it in the 13th.*

The Wildcats, who have their own sterling tradition with four state titles under 27-year head coach Wayne Richardson, survived a potential Jonesboro rally in the seventh inning of the semifinal game when, with the bases loaded and one out, Watson Chapel turned a liner to third into a game-ending double play.[66]

Saturday, May 6, 2006
5A North Little Rock Charging Wildcats
vs.
5A East Sylvan Hills Bears
Quarterfinals of the 2006 State Tournament
@ NLR

Saturday's game against the North Little Rock Charging Wildcats was nothing short of complete devastation. With the stands packed, the energy was electric the entire night. By the second inning, we had deciphered NLR's pitching signs—something we had been good at doing the entire season. We yelled phrases from the dugout to our batters about the coming pitches, and it paid off. Adding to the victory was that *"Hillside's southpaw standout Ashur Tolliver had a career game. The future UALR Trojan turned the anticipated pitchers' showdown between he and North Little Rock's Evan Cox into a no contest by hitting a pair of two-run home runs off the Wildcats ace."*[51] Hunter hit a grand slam, Boles was 2 for 2, and Roark was 2 for 4. We scored thirteen runs in a row on twelve hits following NLR's only run in the second inning. We were invincible that Saturday night at

Vince DeSalvo Stadium. The team could do no wrong.

Monday, May 8, 2006
5A West Fayetteville Bulldogs
vs.
5A East Sylvan Hills Bears
Semifinals of the 2006 State Tournament
@ Lakewood Village

We walked into Monday's game, which was played at Lakewood Village's spare field—a far cry from NLR's stadium, with the same swagger. As the number one seed from the 5A East, we took on Fayetteville, the 5A West's number two seed. We thought we could pull off the same stunt as the previous game and decipher their signs. We were met with a rude awakening. Their assistant coach sat on a bucket, holding up a clipboard to hide the signs coming from the head coach. They saw what we did on Saturday and adjusted, while we didn't.

> *"The Sylvan Hills Bears came up short in their bid to repeat as Class AAAAA state champions. In one inning, Sylvan Hills watched a great season slip away after winning the AAAAA East title and advancing into the quarterfinal round of the state playoffs.*
>
> *Fayetteville (West No. 2) scored 10 of its total 11 runs in the top of the fourth inning in the second round of the AAAAA state playoffs after a questionable call gave the Bulldogs the momentum in the game. Fayetteville gave Sylvan*

Hills (East No. 1) its first shut out and first run-ruled loss of the season, ending one of the favorites for the state crown's chances Monday night at the Don McGee Complex in North Little Rock.

"We can go back and do a lot of 'what if's'," Bears head coach Denny Tipton said. "Did we deserve to win? No. Did they feed off of the call? Yes. We can second guess ourselves all week long, but I still probably would have done things the same. That was the call, and that's how quickly things can change."

The call in question happened in the top of the fourth. Fayetteville scored its first run with one out in the inning after loading the bases. Bulldog substitute runner Collin Sanders came *home on a passed ball, giving them a 1-0 lead and moving Drew Baker to third.*

Tim Carver then bunted into a fielder's choice for Bears third baseman Nathan Van Schoyck. Van Schoyck made the throw to catcher Taylor Roark, who tagged Baker as he approached the plate. The umpire ruled Baker safe, to the dismay of Tipton and the entire Sylvan Hills' dugout. Tipton disputed the call repeatedly, but the run stood, and Fayetteville began a scoring marathon that would span over 40 minutes and three Sylvan Hills pitchers in one inning.

After three-and-a-half innings, starting Bears pitcher Tony Pavan was relieved by Ross Bogard after striking out four batters and giving up four hits and three walks. After giving up two walks and committing an error, Bogard was replaced by Roark three batters later after three more Bulldog runs.

Another walk loaded the bases again for Fayetteville, and a shot to left field from designated hitter Cameron Walker scored two more runs. The Bears gave up one more hit and committed two more fielding errors before finally stopping the Bulldogs' rampage. Fayetteville added one more run in the top of the fifth to set the final margin, before sending Sylvan Hills out after four batters in the bottom of the fifth.

The Bears finished the game with five hits, no runs and five errors. A total of four

pitchers took turns at the mound for Sylvan Hills.
Fayetteville finished with eight hits, 11 runs and
no errors. Sylvan Hills ended the season with a
final record of 22-9.[51]

The Purple Dogs clubbed Sylvan Hills 11-0
in a run-rule abbreviated contest in Round 2. It
was the first time Sylvan Hills had been shut out
all season and the first time the Bears had been
run-ruled in four years.[53]

We were filled with a mix of emotions after the game -
anger, humiliation, and a desire to blame the loss on that one
terrible call. But, upon reflection, we realized there was more to
it. We allowed the call to get to us, and our pitching suffered.
The momentum shifted heavily in their favor, and we eventually
gave up. Our team, which had the potential to replicate the
magic of the 2005 State Championship run, fell just one game
short of reaching Baum Stadium. Despite winning Conference
and being the top seed, it didn't matter.

Fayetteville went on to win the 5A State Championship
in 2006 and the 7A title in 2007, followed by another 7A title in
2008 after we dropped into the 6A classification.

Fayetteville (29-3) advanced to the
championship game after beating North Little
Rock, 6-4, on Monday in the semifinals of the
Class 7A State Baseball Tournament in North
Little Rock. If the Purple'Dogs win today, they'll be
tied for the fourth most state titles (5) in all of the
state's classifications. The only schools with more
than five are Pine Bluff (10), Junction City (7) and

Sylvan Hills (6).[53]

Hats off to them. They completed an incredible four-year run of consecutive titles. To say they were good when they mercy ruled us would be an understatement. We spent the 2007 season playing the "what-if" game, but there was nothing we could do to change what had happened. All we could do was strive to avoid similar circumstances in the future, something we knew we could do. History and depth were on our side.

> *Longtime baseball power Malvern made its 23rd consecutive postseason appearance Friday. Malvern thumped Pulaski Academy, 11-1. Five other tradition-rich schools - North Little Rock (18), Sylvan Hills (17), Batesville (17), Nettleton (13) and Magnolia (12) - have lengthy consecutive streaks as well.*[50]

CHAPTER 9

So far, the Bears, who will take on Watson Chapel for the 6A state title today at 5:30 at Baum Stadium in Fayetteville, haven't had to make any excuses. After all, excuses are reserved for failure, and the Bears have experienced precious little of that this season.

"It's been one of the strangest seasons I can remember," said Sylvan Hills head coach Denny Tipton, now in his 11th year at the Bear helm. "If anything, all of it has brought this group closer. Everything we've been through has helped them develop a team concept. Everyone on this team cares about everybody else. Now, they're just worried about getting it finished."

If they do put the bow of a state title atop this season, it will be the Bears' seventh in baseball, tying them for third overall with Junction City. Pine Bluff is the leader with 10 baseball championships.

In fact, glance through the Arkansas Activities Association record book and you'll see the name Sylvan Hills in just about every category — title game appearances: 11 (third overall); state tournament wins: 60 (a win today would move them into a tie for first overall with Pine Bluff); semifinal appearances: 18 (fourth overall). They already own the record for most state tournament appearances with 38.

Conference titles are well and good, but for a program like Sylvan Hills, success is measured at least by state title game appearances, if not outright championships. Tipton said the two-year hiatus from Fayetteville was tough.

"One of the reasons you do this is to win that title," he said. "So it was important we get back this year. Once you've been there, you like to go back every year. But it takes a little luck along the way."

Where does this Sylvan Hills team rank in school history? Tipton said all his teams have had special qualities.

"But this one has to rank right up there with one of our better teams," he said. "The defense and pitching has been great all year.

We've swung the bat well most of the time this year."

What makes this year a little special, though, are the circumstances surrounding it — the tragedy, tumult and, thus far, the triumph. Tipton won't deny that all of that factors into today's game.

"It's always a goal to get to the state championship," he said. "But we've dealt with so much this year. I can't lie. I think it means something more with everything we've been through."

Watson Chapel's strength would appear to be its pitching. Chance Cleveland and Michael Newby, who both sport 11-1 records, are considered co-No. 1's in the Wildcat rotation. WC assistant coach Chad Cope said both throw in the mid-80s, but that Cleveland had a little sharper breaking ball. He said he wasn't sure as of Friday who would start tonight's game.

"Pitching and defense are definitely our strengths," Cope said. "We've won most of our games 4-1, 4-2. We hit the ball at times, but we haven't hit the ball good consistently. We try to play small ball, move people over."

Cleveland and catcher Nick Cox, a Garden City (Kan.) Community College signee, are among the Wildcats' biggest threats at the plate. Cox also boasts a strong arm.

"Not a lot of people have stolen on him, but

we know Sylvan Hills has a lot of team speed,"
Cope said.[66]

Arkansas sports implemented a 1A to 7A system based on school population sizes in the fall of 2007. The championship game for each class was played in Fayetteville at Baum Stadium, home of the University of Arkansas Razorbacks. Seven games in one day were unrealistic, so they were split between Friday and Saturday. Each year, the divisions rotated down a time slot. Our 6A game was scheduled for the final slot on Saturday night, which would be the final State Championship game of the season.

Friday night kicked off with a bang as 7A Fayetteville took on third-year program Springdale Har-Ber in a matchup of some of the largest schools in the state. Fayetteville, the same team that beat us 3-1 about a month ago while not facing either of our aces, won their third straight championship behind the arm of Taylor Shaddy. Class 1A was next. Taylor beat Trinity Christian 12-2, followed by 2A Woodlawn winning against Dierks by a score of 15-5. Woodlawn's head coach, Tommy Richardson, won his first state championship in his fifteen-year coaching career. His brother, Wayne Richardson, coached the Watson Chapel team that would be taking on Sylvan Hills in the 6A game, hoping to be the first brothers in Arkansas high school baseball history to win championships in the same season.

Class 4A Valley View and Rivercrest jumped the 3A game and played at 10:00 a.m on Saturday. The tightest game of the weekend so far ended with Valley View pulling out a 5-4 win. Harding Academy then beat a sloppy Marmaduke in the 3A championship, 8-4. The Class 5A championship ended with

Harrison beating Malvern, 7-3.

With six games ahead of us, our 5:30 p.m. start time felt forever away, but we were prepared. Tipton wasn't one to give the team something we didn't earn, even with the difficult year. We worked hard, played hard, and as a reward, Coach gave us a little bit of luxury. Well, to an eighteen-year-old kid, it was luxury. That was my thought as the bus rolled up. It wasn't the usual yellow behemoth that Mr. B. drove, where we crammed our gear into the first four or five rows then spread out across the thin firm seats. No, this was different. The charter that rolled up had individual cushioned seats with headrests, what felt like a yard of legroom, an under-carriage cargo space, a television in every row, and even a bathroom. Coach made sure we knew it was number one only back there. Now, we loved Mr. B and his yellow bus, but this was a dream, especially since we were making another three-hour trip. We were just up there a few weeks earlier to face Fayetteville High School and watch the Arkansas Razorbacks play at Baum. This time, it was different. We had bigger things on our minds.

I'm not sure how Coach managed to convince the school, but we hit the road on Thursday to prepare for our game on Saturday. We only stopped for a mass bathroom break where the guys in the back threw away their spit cups before Coach found them. Soon after we settled in, the TVs flickered on, and the opening credits of the movie "300" appeared. I'm not sure whose idea it was, but we all became fixated on the screen. As the bus rolled through the winding Ozarks, each guy on the bus was thinking the same thing: that's us. That's our story.

Looking back on the season, we realized we were much like the 300 Spartans. They faced adversity at every turn, but they never gave up. They pushed through the challenges, and in the end, emerged victorious at the cost of their lives. The comparison between us was not lost. We braved the harshest elements, faced every challenge head-on, and always found a way to beat the odds, taking pride in knowing we had the same fighting spirit as these ancient warriors. We became the Road Warriors, yelling *"No Excuses"* as our batte cry, ready to go to war on any field, against any team, at any time. Determined to win. This time, our sights were set on Watson Chapel. The only question that remained was: would we continue to outlast the trials, or would we succumb to the pressure?

Saturday, May 17th, 2008

6A East Sylvan Hills Bears

vs.

6A South Watson Chapel

Finals of the State Tournament

@ Baum Stadium

After waiting for two days, trying to stay loose and relaxed, it was finally our turn. This was the matchup that the whole state was waiting for, where arguably the two biggest powerhouse teams from the East and South Divisions would finally meet. Baum Stadium was buzzing with excitement for our arrival. We were the 28-6 Sylvan Hills Bears, taking on the 23-3 Watson Chapel Wolves.

The last time Sylvan Hills won a title was against Jonesboro in the 2005 5A Championship. This year's tournament saw Sylvan Hills receive a Bye through the first playoff round and blank Searcy in the Quarterfinals with a final score of 5-0. We did the same to Texarkana's Arkansas High, 3-0, in the Semifinals.

Watson Chapel won their last title in 2000. They edged their way into the championship game this year after winning a thirteen-inning shootout with Jacksonville, 6-5, then defeating a fantastic Jonesboro team on Monday. Both teams defied the odds to make it to this matchup.

We went through our warm up routine in the outfield and ran out to the outer wall as usual. The stadium was immaculate. This was just another road game at a new ballpark for us. Forget everything else and focus. Coach pulled us together as usual to pray for a safe game, protection, and unbelievable sportsmanship. He finished and gave the same encouragement he had from the beginning.

"The only way we lose this game is if we beat ourselves. If we play our game, there's nothing they can do to stop us. Stay calm. Look for your pitch, and drive it. Stack it up. One, two, three, no excuses!"

Watson Chapel was the home team taking the third base dugout. Surprisingly, all six previous matchups were won by the team in the third base dugout. Would that continue? Stepping onto this field for this game was a dream come true for every Arkansas high school baseball player. We knew we had beaten the best of the best, and now we were only one game away from bringing home a championship. The awe of the stadium we had all grown up watching the Razorbacks play in was surreal. The announcer came over the stadium.

For the Sylvan Hills Bears,
#28. Sr. Clint Thornton. Second base.
#3 Sr. Mark Turpin. Left Field.
#24 Sr. Hunter Miller. Center Field.
 #8 Jr. D.J. Baxendale. Pitcher.
#1 Jr. Justin Treece. Shortstop.
#27 Jr. Nathan Eller. Third Base.
#18 Soph. Jordan Spears. Catcher.
#14 Sr. Jake Chambers. Right Field.
#2 Jr. Ty Van Schoyck. Designated Hitter.

#19. Jr. Blake Evans at First base.
Head Coach Denny Tipton.

For the Watson Chapel Wolves,

First. Chase Smith. Center Field.

Second. Landon Hardin. Left Field.

Third. Chance Cleveland. Short Stop.

Fourth. Nick Cox. Catcher.

Fifth. Ryan Derdenne. Designated Hitter.

Sixth. Tyler Massanelli. Right Field.

Seventh. Michael Newby. Pitching.

Eight. Dillon Barker. First base.

And batting ninth. Antowine Jackson. Second base.

Head Coach Wayne Richardson.

As the lineups were announced, and we took our positions on the first base line for the National Anthem, it felt like we were about to engage in the biggest battle of our lives. The sight of our guys' mohawks waving in the wind while singing the anthem created an unforgettable image. Cheers of *"Let's play ball!"* echoed across the stadium as we finished.

The game of baseball hadn't changed. It was the same that day as it was the week before and the week before that. Put the bat on the ball, get runners in scoring position, and score. One run an inning. Coach would tell us that's all it takes for most games. Just one run an inning.

We took positions along the top of the dugout stairs. There was no railing, but we didn't care. We were going to make as much noise cheering our team and distracting theirs as we could.

Clint started us off in the first. He had a good eye, earning a leadoff walk. Playing into that one run an inning strategy, Turpin pushed a sacrifice bunt down the line, moving Clint to second. One out. Hunter took the box in the three-hole and earned a walk. Two runners on. Baxendale's fly to left field failed to move the runners up. Two outs. Coming to bat, Treece was still fresh, recently returning from his broken arm. A curveball in the dirt from Newby got away from Nick Cox behind the plate. Thornton took off for third base, but a perfect throw from Cox sealed the first inning for us. Three outs.

We sprinted to our positions in the bottom of the first, and watched Baxendale mow down the first three batters with two strikeouts and a groundout. 0-0 after one. A quick exchange, and we were back up to bat. The back and forth goose eggs continued.

We countered in the fourth with our first base hits from Turpin and Baxendale. Treece got on by an error, loading the bases for Eller with two outs. It was easy to see that Nathan was pressing. He knew there might not be another opportunity like this. We hoped for a base hit or a passed ball, anything to get a run on the board. Instead, it was a shallow fly ball to left for the third out. D.J. retired eleven straight Wildcats before getting into trouble in the fourth. With two on and two out, we were able to settle down and finish the inning, but something about the game didn't feel right. Four innings and the score remained 0-0.

The dugout was growing restless. Between innings, we jogged down the foul line to stay warm, knowing our chance to make a difference could come at any moment. For every at-bat, I stood at the top of the dugout, watching the windup and timing the pitch, trying to find a flaw we could exploit. The top of the fifth was quiet again. Still 0-0. In a seven-inning game, more than half was over without a single run. It was said that the game would be quick-moving and low-scoring, but for a team that was outscoring opponents three to one, it was difficult to watch our guys struggling at the plate.

Something about that fourth inning for Chapel sparked some confidence against Baxendale. Massanelli got a leadoff single on a high fastball. He caught up. Newby headed to the plate and laid down a bunt right back to D.J. A throw to second to get the lead run calmed the crowd. Ryan Brown pinch-ran for Newby while Cameron Moss stepped to the plate. Miller played deep centerfield because his speed allowed him to get to most shallow balls, but Moss was able to drop one into left-center. Brown moved up to third on the throw while Moss took second. Antowine Jackson, the nine-hole, was up. He showed bunt. *"Squeeze!"* we all yelled. The infield charged, getting ready to make a play at the plate, but Jackson pulled back and lifted one into shallow right. Brown scored, and Moss moved up a base. 1-0. It hurt. Watson Chapel had the lead. It wasn't insurmountable, but it was a lead.

Leadoff Chase Smith stepped into the box next and blooped one over Treece into left field. Moss scored from third, and Jackson moved up to second on the single. 2-0. A couple of Texas Leaguers, and Watson Chapel seemed to have figured out D.J.'s slider. We were pacing in the dugout now, watching Coach Foor's head shake as he looked at the ground. A sacrifice bunt from Hardin moved the runners to second and third. Cleveland lined a ball up the middle. Hunter picked it up after a few bounces and launched it on a rope to home, but the throw was late. Both runs scored. 4-0.

A few dinky hits strung together. Chapel had taken a four-run lead. Baxendale was angry. We could hear him yelling at himself from the dugout. I'm sure the stands could hear him, too. Tipton called time and walked to the mound to calm him down. The visit must have worked because D.J. threw three straight strikes and caught Cox looking for the third out.

The top of the sixth inning and we were down 4 - 0. This wasn't the plan. What happened to the Road Warriors, the 300, the era of *"No Excuses?"* Newby had been pitching well. We couldn't get a hit with runners in scoring position. The game felt over. We were choking, and it was evident that I wouldn't get a chance to contribute on the field. It didn't matter that we were the number two team in the state. Everything we had accomplished up to that point was irrelevant. Heads were down, and murmurs replaced the typical excited cheers as Clint, our leadoff hitter, stepped to the plate for the third time.

"Ball one!" the umpire yelled.

"Good eye. Wait for your pitch, Clint. Watch it all the way," our dugout roared.

Another pitch from Newby, *"Strike!"* the umpire called.

"Alright. Not your pitch. Here we go. Sit back on the curve. Get this one," we encouraged.

Clint adjusted his batting gloves and took a long look down the third base line. Coach didn't give any signs; he just assumed his usual swing level and see the ball stance, hoping Clint would stay calm. Taking a deep breath, Clint got back in the box. Newby was already ready for him. He wound up and delivered a high fastball that Clint hit down the left-field line. The crowd came alive as Coach Foor sent him to second, and Clint slid under the tag for a leadoff double.

"There we go, boys! That's what we needed. Let's keep those bats going! Drive him in, Turp!" we shouted from the dugout.

Mark walked up to the plate, took a practice swing, and looked down to third base for the signs. With no outs, this was our chance to strike back. We needed to cut the score in half. We saw the sign from the dugout: sacrifice bunt. Mark was a great hitter, but small ball made more sense. He had already laid down a perfect bunt in the first inning to move Clint to second, so repeating the process seemed like the right move. Move the runner to third, and let Miller hit him in. Simple.

"*Strike!*" the umpire yelled.

Turp missed. We watched as it went right past his bat. The third baseman was playing even with the bag, and Mark tried to place it but missed. He got the signals again. The same plan. Mark adjusted and put the bat on the ball, laying down a perfect bunt down the first baseline that rolled foul.

With an 0-2 count, Coach couldn't risk another miss. "*Drive something,*" he yelled.

Newby reared back once more. Turpin hit an outside-hanging curveball up the middle past the pitcher. Clint got a great jump from second. Coach was halfway down the third baseline, ready to stop him if Smith fielded it well. Clint rounded third, looking for the ball, and Coach sent him. It was a race to home plate. What was going to get there first, Smith's throw from center or a resilient Thornton? The slide. The catch. Clint touched the outside of the plate and looked to the umpire. "*Safe!*"Finally, the Bears were on the board. Back-to-back hits and we had our first run of the game. Only took six innings.

Watson Chapel's Coach Richardson had seen enough from his starter. A walk to the mound, and it was obvious Newby was coming out. A solid five innings with one earned run against the hottest hitting team in the state deserved a standing ovation from the Watson Chapel faithful. It would be up to the second half of their duo, Chance Cleveland, to take them to the end. Cleveland made the short trip from shortstop to the mound to warm up. In his last outing against Jacksonville, the thirteen-inning duel, Cleveland racked up twelve strikeouts. A quick shuffle of defenders, and Watson Chapel was ready to go again. We watched from the dugout as he warmed up, almost the whole dugout with a bat, timing his pitches. His movements were smooth to the plate, but the scouting report showed his curveball was hit or miss.

Hunter stepped in as Coach gave signals to Turpin at first. First pitch, foul ball to the left side. Getting ready for the second pitch, Mark had a huge lead. Coach hadn't given a steal sign, but Turpin had the green light if he could get a good jump. Cleveland set, one look, two looks, a spin and throw. The move and tag were quick but not in time. Turp got back up, dusted the dirt off his jersey, and then took another lead. Cleveland set, one look, and another throw to first. Mark got back easily. It was clear that Chapel didn't want him moving into scoring position with the heart of the lineup up to bat. For the third time, Cleveland set, but this time, he delivered to home. Miller grounded the curveball to first base. A double play ball, but Turpin was off with the pitch, and Jackson fumbled with the ball, unable to get it to second in time. Miller beat out the play at first to put two on with no outs, bringing Baxendale back to the plate.

This was a dream scenario where you would want to be the guy batting—a time to shine. But D.J. must still have been in his head after the last inning because he struck out looking. Treece was up next and had already put the ball in play twice. With a 2-1 count, he grounded one back to Cleveland on the mound, who turned and threw to second, hoping for the double play. The got the one, but Hunter broke up the play for two.

Treece ran through first without a throw. Two outs with two on, one in scoring position. Eller's bat had been quiet, going 0-2 on the night. Cleveland reared back and blew a fastball by Nathan's swing. Treece had a decent lead at first, but there was no steal sign. It would be a perfect time for a delayed or three-quarter steal, with a hope of Treece getting in a run-down to score the second run, but nothing yet. Another fastball. *"Strike!"* came from the umpire. Cleveland set again. Strike three swinging on a ball in the dirt, Cox dropped it, and Eller took off for third. Mark stopped halfway to home, waiting on the throw. Cox stepped out wide and made the easy throw to first for the third out. The Wolves got out of the jam with a fielder's choice and a couple of strikeouts, keeping the game at 4-1 in their favor.

In the bottom of the sixth, Coach Tipton went to the bullpen, calling on Chris Daulton to replace Baxendale. After giving up four runs and topping ninety pitches, it was the right move to pull D.J. But instead of going with the Bears' number two starter, Hunter Miller, Tipton chose the fireball Daulton. His fastball had great speed, and he even had a decent curve, but Daulton had struggled with control for most of the season. Flyout. Groundout. Groundout. Three up, three down. Chris couldn't have made it look any easier. The sixth was finished, leaving us only one more chance to take the lead.

From the dugout, we could see a line forming at the top of the stadium on the third base side. At the time, we weren't sure what was going on. It didn't matter. We were locked in on the seventh inning. It wasn't until later that we found out the line was for ordering Championship T-shirts for the winning team. A shirt company would take a picture of the team with the trophy after the game and make shirts on the spot for fans to take home. Watson Chapel's fans were already celebrating the victory and ordering their shirts. Our one lonely run through six innings showed on the scoreboard out in right field. Among those fans, J.T.'s mom waited her turn to get to the front of the line. She ordered a couple of shirts and got a ticket with a high order number on it. She was walking away when she noticed the ticket said Watson Chapel on it. A quick turn around, and she was able to get the man's attention. She wanted a Sylvan Hills shirt. I'm sure there were some stares and laughs from the Watson Chapel crowd, but she wasn't leaving until the ticket was corrected. A new ticket was created with the right name, and at the bottom, the number one. Mrs. Long hadn't given up on us, but her hope might have been too little, too late.

We were down to three outs, with our 7-8-9 hitters up to bat. Three outs. It was all that remained in our season, which had been shaped by long practices, tough games, and unexpected catastrophes. It all came down to these final three outs. Coach Tipton called everyone together at the top of the dugout stairs.

"Boys, this is it. One inning. Three outs. One chance. Whatever happens out there, it's been a good run. I want you to look up into the stands. I want you to take a look at your families and friends. They're proud of you. Coach Foor and I are proud of you. Take a deep breath. Let's take it back to the basics. See ball, hit ball. Stack it up. No Excuses, on three."

"One, two, three! No excuses!"

It was our loudest chant of the year. We could feel it deep down. We took off running down the first baseline to pound the wall for Taylor one more time. The crowd gave us a boost of energy as Spears walked to the plate. He was 0-2 on the night, but we couldn't tell. His face was focused as he took his practice swings and adjusted his TR7 sweatband before stepping into the box.

The crowd's noise faded as Cleveland wound up. The umpire's call echoed through the stands. *"Strike!"* A belt-high fastball on the inner half—a dream pitch making the count 0-1. Spears stepped out and took a deep breath then stepped back in. Cleveland started his motion and delivered an inside curveball that Spears lined foul down the left-field line. He could have started the inning off with a double, but instead, the count moved to 0-2. Taking his time, Cleveland set again and delivered. *Ding!* Spears got enough of the ball to get it into the hole at shortstop. No throw to first. We cheered as loud as we could while Coach Tipton immediately called for a courtesy runner for our catcher. Foor looked through the dugout and motioned to Tipton, asking who he wanted. They settled on McKinney, who took over for Jordan.

Chambers walked to the box to get his sign from Coach. We needed three runs, so there was no steal or bunt sign. Everything got wiped off. McKinney took a short lead, and Jake readied himself for a tough at-bat. After a couple of pitches, he lined a single up the middle and moved McKinney to second. Two on, no outs, and us Bears had a rally brewing. Van Schoyck started toward the box, but Coach Tipton moved toward the plate quickly. Ty had looked shaky all night with a strikeout and groundout. It's tough not playing the field while being the DH. I stood at the top of the dugout, looking back and forth between Coach Tipton and Foor. This was the chance I had been looking for - a pinch-hit opportunity to help us extend the game. Bat in hand, I paced the top of the dugout when Foor yelled out, *"Evans!*

Grab a bat. You're up!" My heart sank. I wanted to cheer on Blake as he walked to the plate, but I couldn't bring myself to do it. It had been a year of ups and downs for me, and Coach Tipton, Foor, and the team knew it. But I had proven myself before in tough spots. All the hard work and effort to improve my game felt wasted.

I walked back down the steps as a surprised Evans grabbed a helmet and bat. He murmured to himself as he slid on his batting gloves. It wasn't that Blake was a bad player; he excelled at first base. His height and left-handed glove made him perfect for the position. He could scoop almost anything, but Blake had struggled at the plate toward the end of the season. Hence, the reason Ty was DH for him. Blake walked toward the plate while we did the only thing we could and trusted Coach. Chambers and McKinney took their leads at first and second, respectively. Blake had a weighty stance, heavily leaning on the back leg. Cleveland checked the runners then threw a fastball right down the middle. Evans swung with every ounce of his skinny 170-pound frame. *"Strike!"* called the umpire.

"Keep your head up! See ball, hit ball. Here we go!"

Cleveland wound up again, sending a hanging breaking ball to the plate.

"Strike!"

Another heavy swing, and the count had gone 0-2. Tipton called time and gave a few quick words to Evans before sending him back to the plate. After taking a deep breath, he moved into the box, and the runners took their leads. The pitcher got his sign, and here came the pitch.

"Strike!"

On three straight pitches, Cleveland sat down Evans for

the first out of the inning. As Blake came to the dugout, I met him at the stairs. *"I suck. What was Coach thinking? It should have been you,"* he said, clearly mad at himself.

I felt for him. Coming in cold like that, I've had those moments, and it never feels good coming back to the dugout empty-handed. He threw the bat and helmet against the wall and took a spot on the bench. As a team, we've had moments of frustration throughout the season, but this wasn't the time. We knew that, so we picked him up as best we could and cheered on Clint as he approached the box.

It was Clint who started the rally in the sixth and came around to score. We just needed a base hit to keep things moving. We couldn't let the strikeout affect us. Clint readied himself, Cleveland came set, and McKinney took an extra step away from second base. Cleveland spun and launched a fastball to second base. The tag. Safe. McKinney dove back just in time to keep us at one out. Everyone reset. The pitch from Cleveland. A curveball down and away.

"Ball!"

The runners got the signs again, and Clint stepped back in. Here came the pitch.

"Ball!"

Another low curveball, and Clint was ahead 2-0 in the count. Cleveland looked a little shaken up with McKinney bouncing around second base, ready to take third on a passed ball. Once again, everyone reset. After a long look back at second base, Cleveland turned and pitched.

Bang!

I've known Clint Thornton since I was five years old. His dad, Charlie, coached our Little League teams growing up. We made the All-Star team every summer and traveled around the state after Sylvan Hills Optimist League play ended. He was never the biggest kid on the team, never the strongest, but he was reliable. Clint was a consistent piece playing the best second base anyone could play. It was an art form turning double plays with Turpin and Treece throughout the season. Clint was a good ballplayer, even had a couple of home runs, but he wasn't known for his power. Until today. Until now.

"Go, go, go ball! Go! Home run!"

On a 2-0 count, Tipton gave Clint the green light to put the ball in play. Any base hit would do, but Thornton took an inside belt-high fastball over the left-center field fence. We were mesmerized watching the ball fly. None of us thought it was real. I've never seen Clint hit a ball that far in my life. It was a no-doubter. He was so excited he almost caught up to Chambers while rounding the bases. We rushed to home plate to give him the biggest celebratory cheers and traditional slaps on the helmet. His three-run homer tied the ballgame 4-4. It was this moment that we realized how poetic baseball is. You'll never convince me otherwise. It's not just a children's game. It's more. So much more.

But the job wasn't done yet. We tied the game, but the Wolves would still have their chance to finish things in the bottom of the seventh. We couldn't leave the game in their hands to decide our fate. We needed another base runner. One runner to start things off, and maybe we could put the game away.

Turpin was up, the two-hole with a chance to keep things going. He stepped in the box and took ball one. Cleveland was rattled. Coach Tipton gave Mark the take sign, hoping

Cleveland's nerves would get the best of him. Strike one. No take sign this time, but a look from the coach that it needed to be perfect to swing. Cleveland threw another ball. 2-1 count. A hitter's count. Another fastball, and Turpin was geared up for it. Swing and a miss. Just under the ball. Cleveland wound up and delivered a breaking ball. Mark swung but was too early and missed the ball. Strikeout for out number two.

0-2 with a walk on the night, Miller was our last hope for the seventh. He led the team in home runs. We knew that's what he was thinking. If Clint can launch one out tonight, so could he. He got his pitch. A hanger down the middle. Miller swung but rolled over on the ball. It was a dinky infield grounder for what would be the last out of the inning. But it wasn't. Hunter's speed landed him safe at first base on a bang-bang play.

A single for Miller was really a double. We knew. Watson Chapel knew. The whole ballpark knew what would happen next. First chance he got, Miller is heading to second. Coach had given him a permanent green light for the season, and that wasn't going to change in this moment. Nick Cox, the Mineral Area College commit, behind the plate wasn't an easy target to run on.

Baxendale was up next, but the focus wasn't on him; it was on Miller at first. Cleveland took the mound, set, and expectantly threw over to first base. *"Back!"* we yelled from the dugout. Safe. Cleveland got the ball back for another pick-off attempt, but Miller stayed put at first despite taking a big secondary lead.

"Ball!"

We reset, and Cleveland continued to pick-off, causing the crowd to groan. This time he set, lifted his leg to go home, and as he did, Hunter took off for second base. Cox caught the pitchout and launched a bullet to second base. It wasn't even close. Hunter was safe, and now we had a runner in scoring position.

Baxendale got back in the box and took ball three. Watching the signs, Coach gave D.J. the green light on his 3-0 count. It's nerve-racking when that signal comes because you're so hyped up for a good pitch to swing at that the tendency is to pull your head and either miss the ball completely or roll over, but it's probably going to be the best pitch of the at-bat. D.J. was ready. Cleveland checked on Miller, then delivered a fastball down the middle. Rather than walk the cleanup hitter, the Wolves decided to come right at him. *Ding!* A bloop single into right field.

I don't know if Coach had the stop sign up at third base. I don't know if Hunter was even looking at Coach to see what the call was. I doubt he would have stopped either way. The game was too close. Chances were this would be the last opportunity. The only thing on Miller's mind was: score. Keep running and score. And that's exactly what happened. Miller beat the throw home to score the go-ahead run and put the Sylvan Hills Bears up 5-4 in the top of the seventh. It was a magical moment: Thornton's home run, Hunter's grounder and stolen base, and D.J.'s base hit. The story writes itself. Somehow, the tournament favorite that failed to score through five innings had taken the lead against two of the best pitchers in the state.

But the game wasn't over. There were only two outs, and we had a chance to get more runs. Treece came up next. A passed ball moved D.J. to second base. Treece was intentionally walked to put runners on first and second. Once again, it was Eller up to bat with runners in scoring position. Swinging at the first pitch, he grounded out to first base, ending the top of the inning.

Before we took the field, Coach made some changes. Daulton was done, and Nathan needed to make a quick turnaround from his last at-bat to take the mound. I was excited when I heard this because I thought it meant I'd be taking his spot at third base. That's not what happened. There was a defensive shuffle, and D.J. was sent to third base. It was frustrating. Another opportunity to help my team, and someone else was sent in my place. I remember D.J. saying that he'd never played third base, and that his dad was upset he was put in that position. D.J. had a bright future ahead of him, and getting injured in the hot corner wasn't part of it. Nevertheless, I internalized my emotions and cheered on the best I could.

Eller started off the bottom of the seventh by inducing a quick groundout from pinch hitter Moss to Baxendale at third base. Four pitches later, Jackson struck out looking, taking the Wolves down to their final out. They were back to their leadoff, Chase Smith. With the championship hopes fading, Smith was the one they wanted batting in this position. He settled into the box and took Eller to a 2-2 count. Everyone reset. Nathan entered his windup and delivered a fastball right down the middle of the plate. Smith swung with everything he had. *Ding!*

It was as if the stadium went quiet. I had never experienced anything like it and doubted I would ever feel that way again. Everyone held their breath. All I could do from the dugout was watch Smith send the pitch straight up into the air in foul territory between home and third base. Baxendale ran full speed to a spot, gathered himself under the ball, and slowly started drifting back as the ball moved toward fair territory. Smith was already rounding first base. D.J. reached up and made the catch for the third and final out of the game. That was it. We won. After a four-run rally in the seventh inning, we held off the Wolves to bring home the 6A State Championship.

The dugout cleared as we raced toward the field. D.J. caught the ball right in front of the Watson Chapel dugout. Blake Rix made a beeline for Baxendale, who somehow dodged the speedy Rix to run back toward the pitcher's mound with the ball. The rest of the dugout joined the players on the field for the most energetic dog pile I'd ever been part of. We yelled and screamed. Turpin made grass angels in the infield. Chambers tried to lift Clint onto his shoulders. The cameras swarmed us as we tried to take in every moment of this win. We did it. We actually pulled it off. Our two teams shook hands, and then a huge sign was brought out for a photo op. It felt like we were standing for hours while our families and the media took pictures, everyone excited as we were. We held up the number one and waited for the trophy ceremony. Chris Daulton ended up with the win with his perfect sixth-inning pitching performance. Nathan got the save.

Clint was named Player of the Game, and Baxendale was named Tournament MVP.[59]

It really happened. I'm sure there are details that I missed and parts of the story where I wasn't around to know what happened. I know Mrs. Long got her championship picture shirts. Everyone had to wait forever as that T-shirt group had to stop making the Watson Chapel ones that went to waste to focus on the actual champions. I know that we went through more terrible circumstances than any team should have to endure: the loss of our good friend and teammate Taylor Roack, the destruction of our baseball field and part of the school, taking ground balls off the asphalt parking lot, the seniors finishing our school year at the Recreation Center, J.T.'s broken foot before the season started, and losing his house to the tornado, Treece's broken arm at the beginning of the season, being the Road Warriors, and to cap it all off, the comeback of a lifetime. There couldn't have been a better or more real ending to this season.

Tuesday May 20, 2008

FAYETTEVILLE — "No Excuses"? How about "No Quit," instead?

A season filled with hardship and heartache prompted the Sylvan Hills Bears to adopt a no-excuses credo midway through the season, and they went so far as to emblazon those words onto their T-shirts.

Maybe that was in their minds when they entered the sixth inning of the 6A state championship game on Saturday, trailing 4-0, and facing one of the better pitchers in the state.

But Clint Thornton brought the Bears back from what appeared to be certain defeat with a rousing, game-tying 3-run homer in the seventh inning, and D.J. Baxendale delivered the go-head run with a 2-out single as the Bears held on for a dramatic 5-4 win over Watson Chapel at Baum Stadium. It was Sylvan Hills' seventh state baseball title — their third in six seasons.

"Unbelievable," said Sylvan Hills head coach Denny Tipton, whose Bears endured the death of former player Taylor Roark in January as well as the loss of their field to a tornado in April.

"These kids have been through everything. They just never give up."

Watson Chapel head coach Wayne Richardson, who just completed his 27th year as Wildcat head coach, gave all the credit to the Bears.

"(Baxendale) is a good pitcher and Sylvan Hills is a good ball club," he said. "We played a great team and you've got to make the plays. We didn't get a couple of them and it came back to haunt us."

A game that figured to be a low-scoring pitcher's duel between Sylvan Hills junior ace D.J. Baxendale and Watson Chapel's dynamic duo of Michael Newby and Chance Cleveland, was precisely that through four innings. Goose eggs crept across the scoreboard, with neither team collecting a hit through the first three innings.

But after retiring the first 11 Wildcats, Baxendale suddenly began to run into trouble. He pitched out of a two-on, two-out jam in the fourth, but he wasn't as fortunate in the fifth, when the Wildcats jumped on him for five hits and four runs to take a 4-0 lead. That had to seem like 40-0 the way Newby had mowed down the Bears through the first five innings.

"(Watson Chapel) has an excellent ball club and excellent pitching," said Tipton, who captured his third state title in 11 years with Sylvan Hills. "You know, you're down four with

those two guys on the mound. Watson Chapel had to be feeling good.

"That's why I'm so proud. It's really easy right there to quit. You could say, 'Hey, we're not going to score any runs (against their pitching).' But they battled and battled. That's the key word right there. They never gave up and got the key hits when we needed them."

The Bears got one of those four runs back in the top of the sixth on Thornton's double and Mark Turpin's RBI single to open the inning. That chased Newby for Cleveland. After Watson Chapel second baseman Antwoine Jackson turned Hunter Miller's certain double play grounder into an error, the Bears were in position to get right back in it. But Cleveland got the next three batters, leaving the Bears facing a formidable 3-run deficit heading into the final inning.

Relief pitcher Chris Daulton, who got the win, kept the Bears in it with a 1-2-3 sixth.

Tipton said his club approached the final inning with the right attitude.

"They're a close-knit group," he said. "The last inning, right before they went up there, they just said, 'Let's just finish this thing strong. We started this thing; let's finish it.'"

Jordan Spears beat out an infield single for a promising start and Jake Chambers lined a solid single to center. Blake Evans struck out, bringing the top of the order and Thornton to the plate.

After watching a pair of Cleveland's curve balls miss wide, Thornton got the pitch he wanted — a 2-0 fast ball — that he sent soaring into early evening dusk and onto the hillside beyond the left-field fence.

"He had a real good curve ball," Thornton said. "I was just hoping he'd throw me a fast ball because everyone was saying it was flat. He had been throwing his curve for strikes but we just kept waiting for the fast ball. When he threw it, he threw it right down the middle. I hit it, and that was the best feeling I ever had."

Tipton said he knew from the moment the ball hit the bat that it was a brand new ball game.

"It was gone," he said. "I knew it was gone. I was thinking, game tied. He's been clutch for us all year. Just unbelievable."

That, of course, merely tied the game. And after Cleveland settled down for a strikeout, it was beginning to look like extra innings would be Sylvan Hills' only hope.

But the speedy Hunter Miller beat out an infield hit and stole second.

"I talked to D.J. before I got up to bat and he said, 'Hunter, get on and steal, and we'll do what we always did and I'll get you in and we'll win this thing," Miller said.

Cleveland ran the count to 3-0 on Baxendale, who was granted the green light by Tipton. That proved to be the right decision as

Baxendale, who won the Most Valuable Player award in the game, lined the 3-0 pitch into right center as Miller came around third to score easily and give the Bears (29-6) a 5-4 lead.

"Coach told me to look for my pitch," Baxendale said. "I knew Cleveland was a great pitcher and he likes to come in with his curve ball. I looked away, he threw it away, and I just took it to right just like coach has taught us all year."

Nathan Eller then came in to pitch the final inning. He set down the first two before Baxendale, who had moved to third base, hauled in Chase Smith's pop foul near home plate to secure the win. Watson Chapel finished 23-4.

It was Sylvan Hills' third title in as many classifications over the past six years. The Bears had won the 4A title in 2003, and the 5A title (then, the state's largest class) in 2005.

Next year, they move back down to 4A again, and Baxendale said he sees no reason they won't be right back at Baum, playing for their eighth title.

"We had the motto, 'no excuses,'" he said. "And it just so happened it worked out perfectly this year. From the parking lot practices (the Bears didn't have a field to practice on after the April storms) to dealing with Taylor's death to helping our own player after his house got destroyed by the tornado, we had no excuses. We just had to find a way to get it done, and we finally got it done *in the end."*

Miller, who will head to Ole Miss next fall to play football for Houston Nutt, said it was a rough season, but ultimately, the most fulfilling one.

"We could have given up when we lost a teammate," he said. "But we didn't. We stuck together and came closer as a team when that happened. We're all like brothers now. This is what we wanted. This was our goal: to come up here and win this."[54]

Date	Opponent	Location	Score	Result		Record
2/19	Catholic Rockets.	Little Rock	1 – 2		L	0 - 1 (0 - 0)
2/21	Central Tigers	Little Rock	3 - 2	W		1 - 1 (0 - 0)
2/25	Sheridan Yellowjackets Pather Invitational Tournament	Benton	10 – 1	W		2 - 1 (0 - 0)
2/28	Bryant Hornets Pather Invitational Tournament	Benton	6 – 7		L	2 - 2 (0 - 0)
3/1	Cabot Pathers Red Devil Classic	Jacksonville	8 – 0	W		3 - 2 (0 - 0)
3/7	Beebe Badgers Red Devil Classic	Jacksonville	14 – 2	W		4 - 2 (0 - 0)
	Jacksonville Red Devils Red Devil Classic	Jacksonville			L	4 - 3 (0 - 0)
3/11	North Little Rock Charging Wildcats	NLR	3 – 4		L	4 - 4 (0 - 0)
3/13	Jacksonville Red Devils	Away	9 – 0	W		5 - 4 (0 - 0)
				W		6 - 4 (0 - 0)
3/20	Jonesboro Golden Hurricane*	Home	10 – 0 5 – 4	W W		7 - 4 (1 - 0) 8 - 4 (2 - 0)
3/25	Mountain Home Bombers*	Away	25 – 3 10 – 0	W W		9 - 4 (3 - 0) 10 - 4 (4 - 0)
3/28	Conway Wampus Cats Conway Tournament	Conway	12 – 5	W		11 - 4 (4 - 0)
3/29	Fort Smith Southside Rebels Conway Tournament	Conway	17 – 13	W		12 - 4 (4 - 0)
3/29	Conway Wampus Cats Conway Tournament	Conway	13 – 2	W		13 - 4 (4 - 0)
4/1	West Memphis Blue Devils*	Home	12 – 0 16 – 2	W W		14 - 4 (5 - 0) 15 - 4 (6 - 0)
4/4	Russellville Cyclone	Away		W		16 - 4 (6 - 0)
4/8	Marion Patriots*	Away	2 – 1 7 – 1	W W		17 - 4 (7 - 0) 18 - 4 (8 - 0)
				W		19 - 4 (8 - 0)
4/15	Forrest City Mustangs*	Away	1 – 7 7 – 1	 W	L	19 - 5 (8 - 1) 20 - 5 (9 - 1)
4/19	Fayetteville Bulldogs	Away	1 – 3		L	20 - 6 (9 - 1)
4/21	Searcy Lions*	Away	12 – 0 12 – 9	W W		21 - 6 (10 - 1) 22 - 6 (11 - 1)
4/30	Jacksonville Red Devils*	Away	9 – 4 3 – 0	W W		23 - 6 (12 - 1) 24 - 6 (13 - 1)
5/1	Nettleton Raiders	Away		W		25 - 6 (13 - 1)
5/5	White Hall Bulldogs	Away		W		26 - 6 (13 - 1)
5/9	Round 1 Playoffs - Bye					
5/10	Searcy Lions Playoff Game - Quarterfinals	Texarkana	5 – 0	W		27 - 6 (13 - 1)
5/12	Texarkana Razorbacks Playoff Game - Semifinals	Texarkana	3 – 0	W		28 - 6 (13 - 1)
5/17	Watson Chapel Wildcats 6A State Championship Game	Baum Stadium	5 – 4	W		29 - 6 (13 - 1)

Denotes Conference Doubleheader

There are discrepancies in several dates, scores, and the number of games played due to the chaos of the season. Many games were played on different dates or in different locations than originally scheduled. Two games were played between March 7th and March 25th, with one recorded as a win against an unknown opponent and a loss recorded against Jacksonville, but no known records of the scores has been found The listed game on April 4th against Russellville could not be confirmed with a score. Another game was won between April 8th and April 15th. The opponent is unknown. The scores for the May 5th game against White Hall and the May 9th game against Nettleton could not be determined, but all records indicate that the games contributed to the win column. The final record of the Sylvan Hills Bears was 29-6 (13-1 in conference play).

CHAPTER 10

There is a reason the greatest authors and essayists have more often than not chosen baseball for their topic.

It is a game that lends itself to eloquence better than any of the other sports. Football is a slog through the mud; basketball a frenetic box of chaos. But baseball is graceful and expansive. Just gazing down on an empty diamond settles the mind.

From the crisp dignity of its uniforms to the fluidity of its unimpeded players moving about the field to its languid (literally) timeless pace, it is a game that quietly excites the heart. Football may awaken your inner beast, basketball might *stir the blood into a froth.*

But baseball – when played exquisitely and with just the right dash of drama – has a quality about it that almost has to speak for itself. (Poorly played, by the way, it can be a maddening thing to watch, very nearly an insult to the senses. Which is why, when people ask me my favorite sport to cover, I hesitate to say it is baseball. Yet, it is.)

It is a game that rewards attention to detail. It may be scoreless in the third inning, but did you notice that their pitcher is starting to work behind in the count? That he is starting to leave his curve ball up a little? Aren't the batters starting to make better swings the second time through the lineup?

Perhaps that is why writers have struggled so mightily over the years to capture the soul bliss it can on rare occasion confer upon us.

Last Saturday evening was such an occasion. It was, first of all, an absolutely perfect evening weather-wise. And the panorama of Baum Field and the surrounding countryside hardly hurt matters any.

Then, too, there was this: Watching the field being dragged and smoothed, the crisp white perpendicular lines re-stamped, the plate, the batter's box and pitching rubber brought back to pristine condition, the Sylvan Hills and Watson Chapel players playing long toss, the ball seeming to hang in the air forever, watching the clean, precise movements of the infielders fielding ground balls, the bullet throws across the diamond, hearing the pop of the mitt and the exhortations and praise of the coach, the anticipation of a state championship game, the near-certainty that it would be well-played and probably close as well.

In my six years of writing about sports, there are a few games that stand out, games I'm certain I'll hold on to in memory forever. Who knows? Maybe as my life is flashing past at the end, a moment from one of those games will be among those final images. Hey, I'll take that over a boring seascape or sunset.

I could probably go to my grave with a serene smile if among my last recollections is the sound and sight of Clint Thornton's 3-run home run in the seventh inning on Saturday. As irritating as the ping of an aluminum bat may be, you've never heard such a clean, explosive pop. It was so clean that I don't even recall the usual accompanying reverberations from the contact, just the gasp of the Sylvan Hills fans and the words of a parent behind me: "That baby is gone!"

Then, of course, the roar of the crowd as the Bears, looking all but dead, miraculously, just two outs away from extinction, turned a 4-1 deficit into a brand new ball game.

Was there any way the Bears would lose? I suppose it was possible. After all, as much as writers wax poetic about the game, this was still real life. Nothing was yet ordained and baseball can be as indiscriminate and cruel as any other sport. The Watson Chapel Wildcats will certainly attest to that.

When stunned Wildcat relief hurler Chance Cleveland gathered himself one batter later to record a strikeout, it sure looked as if the Bears would have to win it in extra innings if they were to prevail.

But Hunter Miller beat out an infield hit. Everyone knew the speedy Miller would be on his way to second shortly after he arrived at first. He made it without a throw as the ball got away from the catcher.

Then, with a 3-0 count, D.J. Baxendale got the green light and ripped the go-ahead single into right center. Nathan Eller pitched a three-up, three-down seventh and that was your old ball game – a 5-4 classic that brought Sylvan Hills its seventh state title.

The contest turned out to be an ideal example of one of baseball's great gifts: The reward for patience. A game that began with goose eggs through the first three innings – no runs, no hits, no errors for either team – finished with nine runs and 15 hits.

Though there were two errors in the contest – both by Watson Chapel – there were, thankfully, no unearned runs, which is as it should be in such a game.

So, yes, the poetry that writers so often try to lend to the game of baseball can often trigger the gag reflex. The descriptions, the parallels, can often be contrived and hopelessly overwrought.

But baseball played at its highest level is a wonderful thing to behold. Saturday night, it provided its own poetry.[2]

Coach Tipton called a meeting at the school. Seniors were already out and pending graduation. This was the first time I had been back since the tornadoes hit. We met in the afternoon at the school library, and Coach introduced us to a representative of Balfour who would be making our championship rings. We were given blank pages with ring outlines, books to look through, and Coach Tipton brought his two rings from previous SH titles. The immediate agreement by everyone was that we wanted them big. This ring had to be larger than the other two, no questions asked, and we wanted them to be silver in color. The front was the hardest to decide on. Did we want a trophy or a baseball? The face was going to be huge, so what could cover it well? It was decided to go with a raised SH with blue stones centered inside a bed of clear gems. Down the sides, it needed to say what we won. We were the 6A State Baseball Champs. To personalize them a bit, we had our last name and jersey number imprinted on one side. On the other side, we chose to honor our fallen teammate, Taylor Roark, with the T7R logo. Gone but never forgotten.

We did a commercial for one of the local car dealerships that sponsored us throughout the year, and partially paid for our Championship rings. Coach never said anything at practice, but we knew money had been tight throughout. At the end of every season, Coach would bring us and our families together for a banquet to celebrate accomplishments, give out letters and awards, hand down keepsakes, and send off the senior class. Baskets were made for each senior with pictures and tokens to remember what we had accomplished over our years. It was a time to look back at the year while simultaneously looking forward at the future. The seniors would always pass down something to the next generation of players. It was our way of telling them to keep the dynasty alive. I didn't know what I was going to pass down or who I was going to give it to. It didn't matter because I chose not to go. I was still upset about how the season ended for me. A message from Coach trickled down to me about how disappointed he was that I didn't come and that a player not coming to the banquet had never happened before. But at the time, I didn't care. The banquet was a celebration of a team that I felt I didn't get to fully contribute to.

The same night as the banquet was the first AAA American Legion game of the summer, and I chose to play in it rather than celebrate with the team. I saw it as an opportunity to start over and show Coach Bromley my skills were still there. The hodge-podge team we put together that night at Burns Park didn't fare well. I played left field despite not having played the outfield in years. We lost handily, but my decision paid off. I started almost every game that summer.

Once the rest of our high school talent joined the team, along with some other local stars including some college freshmen returning for one more year of summer ball, we became a menace to play against. There was so much talent that we had to split into two AAA teams. My team made a huge run, and I thought I'd get to play in a championship game, but warming up before our second tournament game, I felt a sharp pain in my shoulder that left me unable to throw. Hitting wasn't as bad, but that moment changed the entire direction of the years to come. I wouldn't find out that it was a torn labrum until after starting my collegiate baseball career at Ouachita Baptist University. Eight months later, after daily physical therapy sessions, I finally had surgery to fix ithe tear. By then, I was so involved with campus life I decided to give up baseball.

That last summer of American Legion ball would be the final time I saw most of our championship team. D.J. would go on to play for the Razorbacks at the University of Arkansas, and my dad and I caught a few of his games. I ran into Hunter a couple of times at the gas station in Sherwood after college, but the rest of the team has been a mystery to me. I haven't seen Coach Foor or Norsworthy, but I have come across Coach Tipton a few times. I returned to Sylvan Hills to watch a game and talked with Coach. We didn't reminisce much, but I recall him saying I was part of an extremely talented group of years for SH baseball. He was right. We won state in 05, conference in 06, 07, and 08, and state in 08. The 09 team was incredible too, with players like Spears, Treece, and D.J. returning. But things didn't stay the same. Coach said if I were a few years younger, I could've been one of the most skilled players on the team. I don't know what that says about those years after I graduated, but it speaks to the talent we had. He could say that for several players, whose playing time evaporated by the end of that season. We weren't just good, we were extraordinary.

> *D.J. Baxendale, Hunter Miller, and Clint Thornton were selected to the All-Arkansas team. D.J. was also selected as the Arkansas Democrat-Gazette's Top Underclassman to watch for the upcoming 2008-09 season after posting a .436 batting average, 12-1 record, and 0.67 ERA.*[55]
>
> *Sylvan Hills' players Hunter Miller, D.J. Baxendale and Clint Thornton were all named All-State. The three Bears were also all named to the All-State Tournament team, while Baxendale was the Most Valuable Player of the state championship game.*
>
> *Thornton still has one more game to play as*

he was named to the East All-Star team to play in Fayetteville this summer.[56]

The main story of the weekend is obviously Sylvan Hills winning the state championship.

- Clint Thornton['s] three-run jack in the seventh inning is the also the obvious highlight, but there are a few other interesting things about these state champs.

- The Bears' last three titles have all been at different classifications thanks to reclassification and a fluctuating enrollment.

- Having an Eller throw the final pitch at Fayetteville should have looked familiar. Nathan's brother Brandon was on the mound when the Bears won in 2005. Middle brother Garrett also got a ring for the Eller family in 2005 as a sophomore.

- Speaking of brothers, Hunter Miller's brother Hayden was also a part of the 2005 state champs.

- Sylvan Hills has the third-most state championships in baseball, while coach Denny Tipton also has the third-most state championships of any head coach. The coach right above Tipton is Watson Chapel's 27-year veteran Wayne Richardson.

- The three wins in this year's State Tournament gives the Bears 61 for the lifetime of the school. That ties Sylvan Hills with Pine Bluff for first place.[57]

T.C. SQUIRES

We are grateful for the blessing you are to us.
As the tassel is turned, a new path you will make.
May God always guide each step you take.
Love
Mom, Dad, Tiffany, Mamaw & Papaw
Vanlandingham and Mamaw Squires

2008

Saturday, September 10th, 2016

Most of us would meet together one last time at Central Baptist Church in North Little Rock after receiving terrible news of the death of Dwight Turpin, Mark's father. In the solemn sanctuary, we gathered to mourn the loss of a great husband, father, baseball player, and coach, who still holds pitching records at the University of Arkansas Little Rock.[58]

I gave Mark, Zach, and Gwynnann the biggest hugs. Blaine Sims, another former SH teammate, spoke about how he would have never gotten his chance to play professional ball without Dwight. Dwight coached all of us at some point or in some way, whether it was on the baseball field, at the practice facility in Maumelle, or in his living room talking about life.

The ceremony honoring the unfortunate end of his great life was one of the last places I saw most of our great team that had solidified a dynasty at Sylvan Hills, a legacy that continues to this day.

As we left the church, I couldn't help but feel a sense of loss. Dwight Turpin had been an important part of our lives and had touched each one of us. It was a reminder that life is fleeting and that we need to cherish the moments we have with the people we love. As we drove home, my mind wandered back to our days playing baseball at Sylvan Hills. The memories flooded back, and I couldn't help but smile at the thought of the incredible team I had been a part of. We accomplished so much together.

We may not see each other often, but the bond we share

is unbreakable. And as I looked up at the sky, I knew that Taylor and Dwight were looking down on us with a smile, proud of the legacy we had created. It's never been just about baseball. We learned so much from each other and from our coaches: dedication, teamwork, perseverance, and especialy about life.

The end of that season marked the end of an era, but it was also the beginning of a new chapter. We grew up together, and now we were ready to go out into the world and leave our mark. It was a time of sadness but incredible joy. We would always carry with us the memories. Life is a journey, and we should never take a single moment for granted. No excuses.

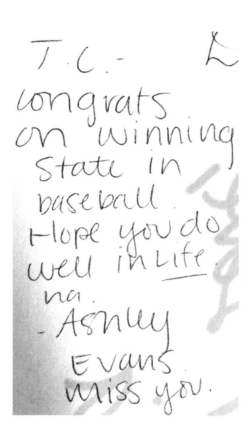

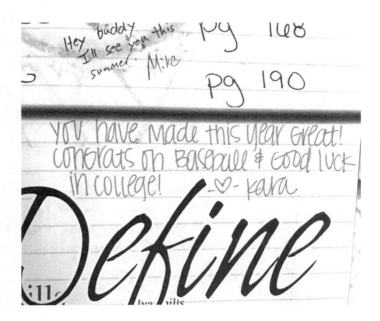

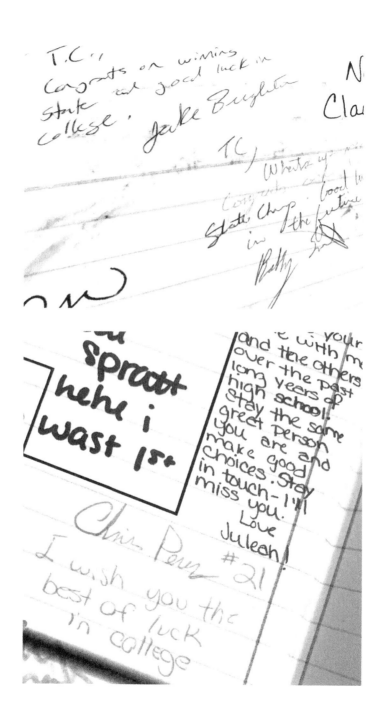

(hahahahaha)

Hey great year! Way to be an individual and not shave your head. Glad you guys ended on a good note! State Champs Daniel J.

HAve a great Summer Man! Had Fun!

C,

k next

Congrats on winning State. Have a great summer.

Have fun at OBU.
—Eric

T.C.
Highschool has been fun with you! Good luck w/ Legion & College!
Love Ya!
♡ Hannah Scott

Congratulations on making it through SHHS and for winning State! I'm glad that I got the chance to get to know you over the past few years. I wish you the best in the future. Take care, and watch out for fields of flowers. Peace...

MR.
GREEN

AFTERWORD

I started writing my perspective on our story in 2012, just a few years after our state championship run. At that time, I still wore my championship ring to significant events and when I visited Sylvan Hills to watch a game or practice. Despite the mixed emotions I felt, I was very proud of what our team had accomplished. As I began piecing together my memories of that season with stories and newspaper articles, reliving the moments of joy and pain was a revealing experience. Fortunately, my parents had preserved several hard copies of the articles because not all of them have been digitized even now in 2023.

This book is not an exhaustive narrative, and there are countless stories and experiences that are not included. If someone wishes to expand upon this story with additional memories or explanations, I would be happy to listen. I tried to be as truthful as possible about my role in the season and the memories of the year, including every emotion, both positive and negative. Writing this story was a way for me to let go of the pain I had felt during the baseball season. Even though the pain was still fresh during the following years as I moved on from baseball, I forgave myself and others for how that season had unfolded. I don't want to diminish anyone else's anguish. We all were devastated by the loss of Taylor Roark. That much is clear.

However, I know there were others on the team who, like me, spent the season watching and waiting for their opportunity. Rix, J.T., Daulton, and Perez, all of whom were in their final year of high school baseball, had some moments of greatness, but I imagine it was not the senior season they had hoped for. I'm sure that each one of them was looking forward to a breakout year that would help propel them into college and beyond. I look back knowing that Coach was just trying to put together the most consistent team that he could. To my knowledge, there was no personal vendettas. We just needed a team that would survive enough games to win a championship, and we accomplished that and so much more.

Almost all of us 2008 graduates pursued baseball during our college years. However, a rule change in the NCAA Division I lowered the maximum number of players on a roster to 35 led most of us to either Division II, III, or Junior College. Clint and Mark found themselves at DIII North Arkansas College, while Hunter moved on to the DI University of Arkansas, then UCA. Blake Rix played for Pulaski Technical College in the NCBA. As for me, I became a walk-on for DII Ouachita Baptist University. I'm not certain where Daulton, Perez, and Chambers ended up playing.

Since 2012, I have attempted to write the story numerous times. However, I was always interrupted by moving to new places, working long hours, or being overwhelmed with emotions while reliving the ups and downs of that season. But now, I've returned to Sherwood, the place I thought I would never come back to. It's 2023, almost fifteen years since we won the state championship. On Friday, March 31, 2023, an F3 tornado tore through Little Rock, North Little Rock, Sherwood, and Jacksonville. For the last five days, I've been cleaning up the debris and fallen trees in my neighborhood and other nearby areas. The damage has been devastating, but just like in 2008, the community has come together to survive. Despite the lack of power, we remain strong and hopeful, even with more thunderstorms on the way.

The tornado hit Burns Park and North Little Rock's Vince DeSalvo Stadium particularly hard. Their equipment shed was destroyed, and all their equipment was scattered across the thirty miles of damage. Jacksonville's Dupree Park was also damaged though not as severely. They will need some work before continuing their season if they get to at all. Wynne, Arkansas, was probably hit the hardest. Maybe this storm will inspire one or all of these teams and their cities to repeat the achievements of the Sylvan Hills High School Bears, 2008 6A Baseball State Champions.

ACKNOWLEDGEMENTS

I would like to extend a thank you to current Sylvan Hills High School Principal Tracy Allen for allowing me to meet on school property to obtain information for this book as well as art educator Stanley Green for providing images and information that would be critical forpiecing together this story.

I want to thank my parents for taking me to countless practices and spending money I know we never had to help me pursue my dream. Thank you to the rest of my family and friends for your part in this journey. And thank you to the many teachers and coaches that shaped me throughout my school years. I am proud to be from Arkansas, an alumni of Sylvan Hills, and a representative of our Lord and Savior Jesus Christ.

APPENDIX

1. Brown, Bonnie. Sylvan Hills High School, Bruin Volume 51. "Define Yourself." Sherwood, Arkansas, 2007, p. 3.
2. Fenton, Kelly. "Sports Reminder: Why It's Still the Greatest." The Arkansas Leader Blog. May 2008. URL: http://arkansasleader.blogspot.com/2008/05/sports-reminder-why-its-still-greatest.html
3. Scott, Hannah. Sylvan Hills High School, Bruin Volume 51. "A Senior Tradition." Sherwood, Arkansas, 2007, p. 6.
4. Jeu, Casey. "Seniors Get Rollin." The Banner, Vol. 38, October 2007, Sylvan Hills High School.
5. King, Jason. "Sports: Wolves Slash Bears Friday." The Arkansas Leader, November 2007, URL: http://arkansasleader.blogspot.com/2007/11/sports-wolves-slash-bears-friday.html
6. Dumas, Ernie. "Editorial: Better Ranking." The Arkansas Leader, January 2008, URL: http://

arkansasleader.blogspot.com/2008/01/editorial-better-ranking.html.

7. McAdams, Abby. Sylvan Hills High School, Bruin Volume 51. "Lunch Junkies" Sherwood, Arkansas, 2007, p. 3.
8. Crise, Doug. "Baseball Report." Arkansas Democrat-Gazette. Sports Section.
9. Harvey, Ricky. "AAAAA expected to be good to last pop." Arkansas Democrat-Gazette, May 14, 2005, p. 30.
10. Harvey, Rickey. "Bears Squeeze Out Sixth State Championship." Arkansas Democrat-Gazette, May 15, 2005, Sports.
11. ArkansasOnline Press Services. "Icy Roads Claim One Life." Arkansas Democrat-Gazette, January 25, 2008.
12. DuBose, Terry. "LETTERS." Arkansas Democrat-Gazette, January 30, 2008, p. 19, Editorial.
13. King, Jason. "Coach recalls Roark as more than a great athlete." The Arkansas Leader, January 30, 2008, Sports.
14. Matchett, Chad. "Roark will play college ball at Henderson State." Sherwood Voice, May 18, 2007, Sports.
15. Roller Funeral Homes. "Obituary for Taylor Kyle Roark." Roller Funeral Homes. Accessed January 2023. URL: https://www.rollerfuneralhomes.com/services.asp?page=odetail&id=12218&locid
16. Reynolds, Andrew. Sylvan Hills High School, Bruin Volume 51. "Reminiscence in Remembrance." Sherwood, Arkansas, 2007, p. 256.
17. "Sylvan Hills hosting baseball skills clinics." Sherwood Voice, January 31, 2008, Sports.
18. Roller Funeral Homes. "Obituary for Billy Joe Blackwood." Accessed: April 2023. URL: https://www.rollerfuneralhomes.com/memorialpage-print-new2.asp?id=61643&locid=32
19. Matchett, Chad. "Sherwood Athletes in College." Sherwood Voice, March 14, 2008, Sports.
20. McAdams, Abby. "Seniors Enjoy Skip Without a Hitch." The Banner, Vol. 38, April 2008, Sylvan Hills High School.

21. Benton, Ray. "Bears Split with Hurricane." The Arkansas Leader, Tuesday, April 17, 2007, Sports.
22. King, Jason. "Bears Take 2 from Jonesboro." The Arkansas Leader, Friday, March 21, 2008, Sports.
23. Daulton, Chris. "Bears Offense Finally Comes To Life." The Banner, Volume 38, April 2008, Sylvan Hills High School.
24. Fenton, Kelly. "Bears Dominate." The Arkansas Leader. April 2, 2008. Sports.
25. Fenton, Kelly. "First Step Toward Baum." The Daily Citizen. May 5, 2007. Sports Section.
26. Benton, Ray. "Bad Luck Buffets SH Bears." The Arkansas Leader, May 9, 2007. Sports.
27. Fenton, Kelly. "2007 state runner-up West Memphis is no match for Sylvan Hills." The Arkansas Leader, April 4, 2008, Sports.
28. Matchett, Chad. "Bears win final home games of the season." The Maumelle Monitor, April 11, 2008 Sports.
29. Hillen, Michelle. "Central Arkansas took 2-twister hit - Heavy rain cited in crash that killed 1." Arkansas Democrat-Gazette, April 5, 2008.
30. Lopez, M., Blankenship, V., & Brown, J. "Weather Causes Extensive Damage." The Banner, Volume 38. April 2008, Sylvan Hills High School.
31. Manthey, T. M., & Howell, C. "Sylvan Hills High classes off for week - Students to be farmed out to other locations because of wind damage." Arkansas Democrat-Gazette, April 5, 2008.
32. Pavlovich, L. Jr. "Tornado Can't Stop This Mentally Tough Team." Collegiate Baseball: The Voice of Amateur Baseball, Vol. 52, No. 8, April 17, 2009.
33. Pavlovich, L. Jr. "Devasting Tornado Doesn't Stop This H.S. Team." Collegiate Baseball: The Voice of Amateur Baseball, Vol. 52, No. 8, April 17, 2009.
34. Matchett, Chad. "Iconic Baseball Park Devastated by Tornado." The Maumelle Monitor, April 11 2008.
35. Hofheimer, J. "School is damaged, students displaced." The Arkansas Leader, April 4, 2008.

36. Reilly, Faith. "Students Return to School." The Banner, Volume 38, April 2008, Sylvan Hills High School.

37. McCoy, J., & Komor, T. "Schools Regroup after Disruptions." The Arkansas Leader. April 12, 2008.

38. King, Jason. "Bears Forced to Road." The Arkansas Leader, April 8, 2008, Sports.

39. Crise, Doug. "Baseball Report." Arkansas Democrat-Gazette. April 6, 2008, Sports.

40. Crise, Doug. "Baseball Report." Arkansas Democrat-Gazette. April 13, 2008, Sports.

41. Conley, Fred. "Bears drop first conference game." The Maumelle Monitor, April 18, 2008. Sports.

42. Allen, Heath. "Bulldogs nip Sylvan Hills team, continue school-record streak." Northwest Arkansas Times, April 20, 2008. Sports.

43. Fenton, Kelly. "Bears take two from Devils." The Arkansas Leader, May 2, 2008. Sports.

44. Crise, Doug. "Parking lot powerhouse - Sylvan Hills (26-6) overcomes death, destruction." Arkansas Democrat-Gazette. May 9, 2008.

45. Staff. "High school state tournaments." Arkansas Democrat-Gazette. May 8, 2008. Sports. p.29.

46. Staff. "Searcy claws past Wolves." The Daily Citizen. May 10, 2008. Sports.

47. Staff. "Searcy falls to Bears, 5-0." The Daily Citizen. May 11, 2008. Sports.

48. Matchett, Chad. "Semifinal game provides tons of tradition." The Maumelle Monitor. May 16, 2008. Sports.

49. Matcheet, Chad. "Thrilling win, crushing loss for Devils." The Maumelle Monitor. May 16, 2008. Sports.

50. Taylor, Kevin. "7A-West, 5A-West Have Strong Showing." Times Record. May 12, 2008. Sports.

51. King, Jason. "Bears won't repeat." The Arkansas Leader. May 10, 2006. Sports.

52. Allen, Heath. "Purple Dogs set for title clash with Conway." The Northwest Arkansas Times. May 12, 2007. Sports.

53. Allen, Nathan. "Purple Dogs Going For Third Straight Title." Morning News of Northwest Arkansas. May 15, 2008. Prep Sports.
54. Fenton, Kelly. "No excuses needed." The Arkansas Leader. May 20, 2008. Sports.
55. Crise, Doug. "Not a quote - Bigham looks for impact at UA - Overarchieving Texarkana star 'the whole package." Arkansas Democrat-Gazette. June 15, 2008. Sports. P.36.
56. Matchett, Chad. "Several Bears, Owls earn postseason honors." The Maumelle Monitor. May 30, 2008. Sports.
57. Matchett, Chad. "Sideplots from the state champs." The Maumelle Monitor. May 23, 2008. Sports.
58. Griffin Leggett - Rest Hills. "Obituary for Dwight Dale Turpin." Arkansas Democrat-Gazette. September 8, 2016. Accessed April 2023, URL: https://www.arkansasonline.com/obituaries/2016/sep/08/dwight-turpin-2016-09-08/
59. Matchett, Chad. "State champions once again." The Maumelle Monitor. May 23, 2008. Sports.
60. Walker, Nick. "Reddies catcher dies on icy Interstate 30." Arkansas Democrat-Gazette. January 26, 2008. Sports. P.28.
61. Patrick, Rob. "Hornets reach finals of Panther Invitational." Bryant Times. February 25, 2008. Sports.
62. Fenton, Kelly. "Sylvan Hills sweeps Lions." The Arkansas Leader. April 22, 2008. Sports.
63. Fenton, Kelly. "Miller fleet infield, free with bat." The Arkansas Leader. April 25, 2008. Sports.
64. King, Jason. "Bears begin quest for Baum today." The Arkansas Leader. May 9, 2008. Sports.
65. Fenton, Kelly. "Bears bound for Baum." The Arkansas Leader. May 13, 2008. Sports.
66. Fenton, Kelly. "Back on familiar ground." The Arkansas Leader. May 16, 2008. Sports.

As follows, credit for images is given to the photograher where known. Unknown photographer image credit is given to the publication and/or the person who thereby distributed the image. For corrections to image credit or submission of additional images for use in later editions, please email the corresponding address in the copyright section this book.

Beth Hall: p. 55, 57
Bonnie Brown: p. 38
Bruin Vol. 51: p. 1, 23, 41, 43, 44, 45, 47, 48, 81, 133, 258, 259, 260
Casey Jeu: p. 3, 21, 30, 94, 96, 99, 116, 132, 170, 186, 191, 196
Chad Matchett: p. 67, 70
Christy Seawood: p. 39, 46
The Voice Of Amateur Baseball: Cover, p. 146, 147, 156
Danielle Spratt: p. 40, 135
David Parker: p. 73
Google Maps: p. 9, 11, 12, 23, 37, 104, 107
Kara Walters: p. 45
Kayla Bradford: p. 261, 262, 263
Kim Squires: p. 27, 101
Lindsay Hunter: p. 6
Lisa Roark: p. 76
Monty Squires: p.32
Phil Begin: p. 2, 65, 109, 111, 118, 123, 164, 183, 184, 214
Prentice Dupins: p. 138, 142
Stanley Green: p. 83, 163, 269
Stephen B. Thornton: p. 189
T.C. Squires: p. 8, 15, 16, 17, 18, 19, 20, 21, 26, 27, 28, 35, 36, 60, 62, 63, 82, 91, 124, 125, 129, 159, 179, 182, 197, 211, 220, 245, 253, 265, 266, 267, 275, 276, 277

Made in the USA
Columbia, SC
25 June 2023

19237018R00163